STUDY CIRCLES

· ·

A report on this long-standing phenomenon
in adult education as it has been integrated
into Swedish national life and is now being
applied in North America.

STUDY CIRCLES

· ·

Coming Together
For Personal Growth
And Social Change

LEONARD P. OLIVER

Seven Locks Press

PUBLISHERS

Washington, DC/Cabin John, MD

157591

Library of Congress Cataloging-in-Publication Data

Oliver, Leonard P., 1933-
  Study circles.

  At head of title: To understand is to act.
  Includes index.
  1. Adult education—Sweden. 2. Forums
(Discussion and debate) I. Title. II. Title: To
understand is to act.
LC5256.S8043   1987   374.9'485   87-12874
ISBN 0-932020-47-X (pbk.)

Manufactured in the United States of America
Design by Lynn Springer
Typography by the Writer's Center/Dan Johnson
Printed by McNaughton & Gunn, Ann Arbor, Michigan

SEVEN LOCKS PRESS, Publishers
P.O. Box 27
Cabin John, Maryland 20818
301-320-2130

*Dedicated to the living memory
and example of Olof Palme.*

CONTENTS

157591

FOREWORD

David Mathews

PRESIDENT, KETTERING FOUNDATION

In June 1985, I led a delegation from the Kettering Foundation on a study visit to Sweden at the invitation of the Swedish government and the Swedish Institute. We were able to meet with an impressive list of people, including members of Parliament, high-ranking ministry officials, leaders of the national educational associations, and university professors.

The Swedish people seem to be a step ahead of us in the adult education movement in their insistence on the essential link between adult learning and the problems and issues adults face daily. Their nationwide network of study circles, folk high schools, municipal courses, and other forms of adult education effectively enables average citizens to understand and participate more fully in the life of their communities and their nation.

We visited Sweden with a particular interest in their study circles and in other means Sweden uses to involve citizens in public life. We came away impressed with the Swedish commitment to public learning, a commitment shared by both public officials and lay citizens. We marveled at the Swedish penchant for maintaining organization while trying to keep complex bureaucracies responsive to the public interest. We applauded Swedish efforts to broaden the base of study circle participants by providing incentives to the national educational associations to reach out to the new immigrants, rural dwellers, and the undereducated—adult civic education with an underlying social purpose.

At the Kettering Foundation, we also have a strong interest in science and technology policy as it affects

the public, so we were intrigued by the *Kalla Series*
(print materials on scientific issues illustrating the various choices available to the public) and took away
some ideas on how to duplicate it in our own country.
We also gained fresh insights into other important
areas of concern—namely, adult functional illiterates
and tested methods to reach them in civic education
programs, as well as ways to encourage university
faculty to take the lead in the civic education movement
in the United States, both on campus and off.

Since the Kettering Foundation, along with thirteen
other national organizations and foundations, helped
to design the National Issues Forums, a national public
issue program sponsored by the Domestic Policy Association, we were eager to draw parallels between
our two countries' diverse cultural and educational systems, linked philosophically by our mutual interest in
public learning theory. The nationwide debate in Sweden in 1979 through the study circles and the subsequent national referendum on nuclear power development both stand as models for obtaining "public
judgment" on a major issue and for bringing the public
to the policy-making arena. We have learned from
these examples.

In this report on his visit to Sweden, Dr. Leonard
P. Oliver, staff associate of the Kettering Foundation,
examines many of these topics in great depth. His
interviews provide firsthand testimony on how the
Swedish study circles work, how they have contributed
to Swedish society, and what happens when they fall
short of their objectives. His report represents the
most comprehensive examination of the Swedish study
circle phenomenon available in English, providing a
unique glimpse into how another culture's learning system can meet the desires, needs, and interests of its

adult population in a dramatic and extensive nationwide program.

Yet Len Oliver's document goes beyond analyzing
the Swedish study circle phenomenon. He provides a
useful capsule review of our own history of public
forums and small group discussions, and he then offers
two case studies on how the study circle concept, borrowed from Sweden, has been assimilated into the educational programs of an international union and a new
national organization for public issue discussion. By
testing the study circle idea in a pilot series done in
the summer of 1986 for rank-and-file members, the
International Union of Bricklayers and Allied
Craftsmen has demonstrated how union democracy can
be extended to the membership through the study circle format. And through its adoption of the study circle
format, the National Issues Forums program has
gained a simple, effective, and manageable means to
enhance citizen discussion of public issues, particularly
when the format is used in local communities to complement larger NIF programs. Thus, we now have
two dramatic examples of how this Swedish import
can give additional meaning to our own democratic
principles. We anticipate more examples in the years
to come.

We have learned much from our colleagues in these
two visits, and as Len Oliver indicates, we have
evolved a new set of standards by which to judge our
own efforts toward social justice and small-scale democracy. I believe the people we talked to were equally
as interested and curious about how the study circle
can work in another culture. This publication contributes to that cross-cultural understanding by dem-
onstrating that we can learn from each other. We are
both richer for the experience.

ACKNOWLEDGMENTS

No publication is the effort of one person, and this report on the Swedish study circles and their introduction into our adult education practice is no exception. Fred Hoehler, at the time director of the George Meany Center for Labor Studies, and Lisa Portman, former assistant director, invited me to deliver a presentation on cultural policy in the United States on 22 November 1982 as part of their "Scandinavia Today" program at the center. At the session, Lars Ulvenstam, then cultural counselor at the Swedish Embassy, brought the Swedish Bicentennial Fellowship program to my attention. The session also introduced me to many Swedish friends, whom I then had the occasion to interview in Sweden after winning the fellowship. We developed some lasting cross-cultural friendships.

I want to thank David Mathews, president of the Kettering Foundation, for encouraging me to apply and then providing financial support during my stay in Sweden. Ulf Lundin, a friend and another former cultural counselor at the Swedish Embassy, gave me many good leads and ideas for the visit. Marna Feldt of the Swedish Information Service in New York was always pleasant and knowledgeable in response to my numerous questions. John Walldén of the Swedish Consulate General's Office at the Swedish Information Service in New York has been most helpful in his intercessions on behalf of the publication with the Swedish Institute in Stockholm.

Labor colleagues helped, such as Art Shy, director of education for the United Auto Workers, who generously loaned me his notes from his journey to Sweden two years earlier, and Norman Eiger, director of the Labor Education Center at Rutgers University, who provided extensive background material from his own study circle research. Norman Kurland of the New York State Study Circle Consortium offered valuable insights and encouragement. Budd Hall of the International Council for Adult Education based in Toronto provided a list of valuable contacts from his own travels to Sweden, as did Alex Charters, professor of adult education at Syracuse University, and Edmund Gleazer of Washington, D.C.—both old friends.

I am indebted to Anders Clasen, Monica Fägerborn, and Cecilia Reimers of the Swedish Institute, who cared for me and my schedule at every step, and to Ove Svensson, who has handled the extended negotiations across the Atlantic Ocean. I applaud Jon Rye Kinghorn, national coordinator for the Domestic Policy Association, who first encouraged the integration of the study circle into the National Issues Forums network, realizing the potential of the idea for local conveners. I also want to thank Robert J. Kingston of the Public Agenda Foundation for his collegial guidance and support over many years together. Especially deserving are local NIF conveners Anita Fonte (Tucson), Carl Eschels (Grand Rapids), John Buskey (formerly of Lincoln), Ray Gildea (Starkville), and others who pioneered in adopting the study circle idea in their local forums.

I congratulate John T. Joyce, president of the International Union of Bricklayers and Allied Craftsmen, who had the inspiration to attempt to build study circles into an international union's education program, a first for North America. Michael Maccoby, director of the Project on Technology, Work, and Character, who is familiar with the Swedish study circle movement, has been avid in his support for introducing the idea into the Bricklayers' International Union and has given the new program constructive insights at critical times. And Tom Donahue of the Bricklayers, friend and colleague, was instrumental in helping launch the program.

Above all, I want to thank the people in Sweden who consented to be interviewed, who took me to lunch, who told me of sights to see and places to visit, and who provided the substantive insights and comments that have made this publication possible.

Support for this publication comes from the Kettering Foundation and its editorial committee along with Robert Daley, director of public affairs; from the Swedish Institute; and from Calvin Kytle, publisher of Seven Locks Press, who saw in the manuscript an opportunity to contribute to an understanding between our countries as we find ways to collaborate and be enlightened in our search for international peace and justice. I believe the manuscript was vastly improved by the deft and diligent hand of Jane Gold of Seven Locks Press, a dedicated and easy-to-work-with colleague. And I am grateful to Deborah Witte, who provided continual professional support and flexibility in her position as librarian at the Kettering Foundation. Finally, I appreciate the tolerance and quiet support of Eleanor, Erika, and Britt, who were always there when needed.

INTRODUCTION

On my visit to the Brunnsvik College (folk high school) in Ludvika, Sweden, in spring 1984,[1] Brunnsvik's director Torbjörn Strandberg told me that "folkbildung [adult education] is our religion, . . . it is what matters to us." In Sweden, a country slightly larger than California with 8.3 million inhabitants, including more than 6 million adults, roughly a third of the adults are engaged in some form of adult education annually. Given this proportion, it seemed that everyone I met was indeed organizing, leading, or participating in a structured learning experience.

The study circle, now almost a century old, is by far the most popular form of adult education in Sweden. In 1983, for example, one of every five adult Swedes either led a study circle or joined one. By official government counts, there are about 325,000 officially reported study circles conducted annually, with the 2.9 million participants, many of whom are repeats, studying everything from civic affairs to ceramics to literacy for immigrants. The concept is fully integrated into Swedish life and culture, and it has become a model copied by other countries. Study circles are also found throughout Scandinavia, in a few European countries, and, to some degree, in Third World developing countries to combat illiteracy, undereducation, and lack of civic competency.

The Swedish study circles are sponsored by ten national educational associations (see chap. 2), which receive substantial annual subsidies from the national government for their study circle activities. Other formats for adult education in Sweden include 140 folk high schools (residential adult education programs), university short courses, correspondence study, distance learning (telephone, television, radio) carried out through the universities, employers' courses at the work site, and an enlightened program of labor market training for the about-to-be and long-term unemployed. Often a form of the study circle is used in tandem with one of these other formats (e.g., some labor market training takes place in study circles).

I went to Sweden to examine the study circles firsthand—how they are organized and how they train leaders, recruit participants, and use materials. I focused on their use for discussion of public issues—"civic affairs" as the Swedes call it; "adult civic education," "civic education," or "civic literacy" as we know it here.

Over the last few years, in my work for the Kettering Foundation, I have been involved in the development of a national public issue discussion program, the National Issues Forums, sponsored by the Domestic Policy Association. The DPA/NIF is now entering its sixth operational year, with more than two hundred local forum conveners in almost every state who conduct forums each fall on three pressing national issues. Some of the recent topics addressed include "Welfare: Who Should Be Entitled to Public Help?" "Taxes: Who Should Be Paying and Why?" "Immigration: What We Promised, Where To Draw the Line?" and "Crime: What We Fear, What Can Be Done?" All are highly debatable, often volatile front-burner issues.

Since several local DPA/NIF programs were beginning to use the study circle format in their community forums in 1984, my visit to Sweden, the birthplace of the modern study circle movement, was designed to provide us with some insight into this widespread, long-running phenomenon. The Swedish philosophy of adult learning is fundamental to understanding the Swedish study circle movement. Education's practical role is as an instrument for improving and enriching individual and community life; adult education in this sense is conceived as a link between learning and life, based on the individual's innate desire to learn and grow. The Swedes are fiercely committed to the use of adult education for social change.

Brevskolan, the labor-oriented publishing house for study materials, provides the following introduction to study circles:

> The aim of the study circle can be defined as "greater understanding" or insight. Through their studies the members must be enabled to put their lives into perspective and to view their own subject in a wider social context. . . .
>
> [T]hrough their studies the members of the study circle must learn how to come to grips with problems and how to work out solutions in the situations which will confront them later on and which neither the producers of the study material, the study circle leader, nor the members themselves can forecast "today."[2]

Thus, the starting point for a study circle must be the problems adults face. The methods and materials selected should encourage a cooperative atmosphere, with everyone participating on equal terms. Brevskolan calls the study circle "the most efficient form of adult education," and goes on: "The philosophy of the study circle implies that knowledge cannot become living and important until it corresponds to a personal need. No two study circles are alike, nor should they be."[3]

Further, the Swedes strongly believe that adult education should be voluntary, democratic, and participatory, with educational methods chosen to enhance freedom of choice, exchange of ideas, critical thinking, leadership, and application of knowledge to everyday life. Linked with the Swedish passion for active, informed citizens and the nation's concern for social democracy, the study circle from inception has been a natural vehicle for adult civic education. As Olof Palme, the late prime minister of Sweden, said in 1969, "Sweden is to a considerable degree a study circle democracy."[4]

Adult education is obviously fundamental to Swedish life, especially programs that further social equality and social justice, and seek to redress imbalances in the educational attainment of adults. For this reason, study circles are popular; they help remove the impediments to education for many adults who have been away from formal classroom experiences for many years, and they create opportunities for individuals to come together in community and neighborhood centers, union halls, factory work sites, public libraries, and other familiar settings to enrich their personal, working, and civic lives. Few Swedes I met talk about adult education in philosophical or theoretical terms. They take great pride in the application, in doing it, and study circles are among their proudest achievements in practical education for adults.

I visited Sweden to find out how the study circle idea originated there, how study circles are used to promote adult civic education, and how they have evolved into a permanent national institution. The research findings are based primarily on 28 interviews with government officials, directors of several national educational associations, trade union and political party leaders, and former public officials (see appendix). The interviews were supplemented by literature available from the Swedes and written in English, and by articles written by previous visitors from the United States.

1

· ·

Roots in Popular Movements

Study circles, more appropriately "home study circles," were sponsored in the United States as early as the 1870s by the Chautauqua Literary and Scientific Circle in New York, a spin-off of Bishop John H. Vincent's Lake Chautauqua Assembly founded in 1874. The CLSC initiated a popular program of four-year correspondence study with home study circles—organized group reading and discussion—for adults who had no training beyond high school, many of whom, such as women, were denied access to higher education. By 1915, the CLSC claimed seven hundred thousand correspondence enrollees and fifteen thousand study circles, using Chautauqua texts and other publications in these "colleges for one's home."[1]

During the latter half of the nineteenth century, Sweden's adult education movement consisted of private liberal philanthropy dedicated to uplifting the educational levels of the populace primarily through lectures, religious education for adults, workers' institutes and lecturing associations, and liberal-radical professors lecturing to working-class people. But these programs were "sporadic and too tame," according to Peter Engberg of the National Swedish Federation of Adult Education Associations (SFHL), who pointed out that the new popular movements—temperance, trade union, cooperatives, and the Social Democratic party (SAP), all of which were outside mainstream political and social life—were anxious to conduct their own adult education on basic economic and political questions and were searching for a convenient, non-threatening, highly participatory democratic format.

So it fell upon Oscar Olsson, a leader in Sweden's temperance movement, to develop the study circle as a means of popular adult education; later he would be known as the "father of the study circle." According to Henry Blid of Brunnsvik College, Edvard Wavrinksy, an ardent temperance advocate, visited Lake Chautauqua in 1893, was impressed with the CLSC home study circles, and wrote an article about them. By 1902, Olsson had picked up on the idea and organized a series of study circles within the temperance movement. Other socially conscious movements quickly followed suit, among them the SAP, the blue-collar trade unions, the consumer cooperatives, and the free or nonconformist church movement (all founded in the late 1800s), for which study circles provided an effective means of recruiting and educating their members.[2]

Thus, the study circles arose in the bleak conditions facing late nineteenth-century Sweden: a poor, underdeveloped nation unable to support its growing population and burdened with large-scale social and economic inequalities, rural poverty, rigorous living conditions, high rates of illiteracy, and threats of social unrest. Further, between 1840 and 1920, Sweden lost one-third of her population through immigration, with most sailing for the United States. The popular movements acted to overcome these formidable obstacles, with Olsson leading the way in his struggle for working-class democracy:

> Great education work can be carried out with the set-up as proposed here. . . . Shall anything substantial be done *for* this class, this must also be done *by* it.[3]

By 1920, the temperance movement, the free church, and the blue-collar unions had recruited over one million members. The rise of the industrial unions also brought a concomitant growth in the SAP, which strove to bring workers into the political process. All these movements were characterized by lively local organizations, often with their own member-built meeting halls. According to Engberg, this was in keeping with an old Swedish tradition, the "Hemgårds" (houses of discussion) movement—public centers that existed for a time alongside the study circles to encourage cultural/intellectual pursuits removed from political activity. These public "houses" were eventually eclipsed by the popular movements and their study circles.

The study circle, therefore, was a natural vehicle for the popular movements to advance their causes among the people, to create educational opportunities for adults who previously had limited access to formal education, and to teach their members about the organization. The study circle also taught members how to participate democratically in a community or organization, and it brought to the surface new local leadership from circle members. What was learned in the study circle subsequently carried over into political life, as most of the popular movements eventually became active in political affairs.

The basic character and organizational profile of
Swedish popular education were established in the first
two decades of the twentieth century. For example,
the formation of ABF, the Worker's Educational Association, initiated in 1912 by the labor unions, the
SAP, and the consumer cooperatives, gave workers
their own national educational association. Richard
Sandler, founder of ABF and former Swedish prime
minister, talked about worker education:

> The object of workers' education is to turn the
> workers into active citizens in the living cultural
> society. . . . These study circles supply the de-
> mands for self-activity, as they build . . . on the
> free choices of courses of studies. . . . Between
> liberty and guardianship there is no compromise.[4]

But worker study circles also needed quality materials, and Brevskolan was founded in 1919 to meet this
need. Beginning with correspondence materials,
Brevskolan gave study circle participants access for
the first time to quality materials geared to their level
of education and interests. According to Rolf Theorin,
head of the Central Organization of Folk Parks, with
Brevskolan materials and ABF sponsorship, study circles encouraged workers "to gain the knowledge necessary to master public issues, to understand how society
works, to take control of their lives, and to master the
tools to change society." Theorin then commented on
the political implications of study circle activity: "Even
the study circles concentrating on cultural pursuits
helped to bring the workers together, and all this activity resulted in 1932 in the formation of Sweden's
first labor government under the SAP."

The other national educational associations that conduct study circles were established with ABF as a

model, drawing their support from the churches, the YMCA-YWCAs, university extramural departments (Folk University), temperance groups, political parties, and consumer-environmental groups. From their inception in 1902, study circles offered Sweden's undereducated adult population an opportunity for insights, understanding, and skills that were not available through the formal school system. They initially met in homes, churches, meeting halls—wherever people could gather in private—usually without a formally trained leader and with limited materials, sharing ideas and experiences in a democratic atmosphere. And they flourished, with each of the national associations adopting the study circle as its primary mode of communication and education for both its members and the public. Regardless of sponsorship, study circles encouraged self-directed learning and full participation, blending the intensive, small group format with traditional Swedish culture—particularly small-town life and the face-to-face conversations of friends and neighbors. "Democracy is born in conversations," as David Mathews, president of the Kettering Foundation, put it, and nowhere did this ring truer than in early twentieth-century Sweden.

Study circles continued to grow, and by World War II they were the most important form of adult civic education in Sweden. After the war, study circle activities became extensive among members of popular movements, political parties, religious groups, YMCA-YWCAs, university extramural departments, and the public at large. The Swedish government recognized and formalized the practice and organizational structures of study circles in 1947 by introducing government grants to subsidize the costs of leader salaries and materials. The grants went exclusively to the ten

national educational associations; no new association
has been added since 1947.

With government grants came a codification of the
rules for the study circle, which was officially defined
as "an informal group which meets for the common
pursuit of well-planned studies of a subject or problem
area which has previously been decided upon."[5] The
rules were simple and have changed only slightly over
the years. The government subsidies today cover about
40 percent of the costs of the study circles, with the
remainder coming from municipal grants and participant fees.[6]

Since 1947, the number of study circles and participants has grown at an annual rate of at least 10 percent.
The ten national associations actively continue to promote study circles throughout Sweden, and with government subsidies based on total study circle hours,
there is intense local competition among them for
participants. But there have always been enough participants to go around. When, for example, a new
Swedish law in 1962 extended the required years of
schooling from six to a compulsory nine, a generation
of adult Swedes found themselves lacking three years
of formal education. Many turned to the study circles
to obtain the equivalent of the extra school years, much
like our own general educational development (GED)
programs, and this enabled these "second chance adults"
to return for education beyond the high school level.

In recent years, the national associations have been
offered additional government grants as incentives to
create study circles that reach rural areas, the handicapped, the aging, and the new immigrants. Subsidies
are also available for circles that reach housewives in
residential areas.

Most of the ten national educational associations that sponsor study circles today have been around for at least fifty years, and they offer a broad range of subject matter in their study circle programs. But study circle content has actually changed over the years. From their initial efforts to increase literacy and civic/political competency, study circles gradually took on historical, literary, cultural, and language themes. Study materials from the associations were supplemented by materials from the "People's Libraries," created throughout Sweden by the temperance groups and labor organizations long before municipalities extended their library resources outside the cities. Today, the national associations increasingly emphasize cultural studies (languages, literature, the arts) rather than the political, social, and economic issues (civic affairs) that dominated study circle content earlier. Sweden has become an educated, middle-class, relatively affluent society, and her adult education interests obviously reflect this status.

However, the changing content of the study circles toward artistic, crafts, cultural, and travel programs has some national association officials concerned. Most of those interviewed pointed out that their circles still emphasize civic affairs, but as Patrick Breslin of ABF observed: "Much of this is more in the form of information flows from the parties, the unions, and the national associations than frank discussion of public issues. It is a form of political education."

Still, the government, with a continuing interest in promoting study circles that deal with public issues, has provided additional subsidies over the last few years as incentives for "priority circles"—study circles and materials on civic affairs. Both the government and the associations seem to be wrestling with the

conscious use of the study circle format to enhance
civic competency—one of the seminal ideas that stimulated the introduction of study circles nearly a century
ago. A national referendum on nuclear power in 1980,
recent national concerns over the influence of the computer on Swedish society and over environmental deg-
radation, and similar national issues have served to
increase attention in the study circles on civic affairs.

2

. . . .

Sponsorship
And Organization

Sweden has ten national educational associations, which promote, organize, and conduct study circles with government subsidies:

ABF   Arbetarnas Bildningsförbund [Worker's Educational Association]

FS   Frikyrkliga Studieförbundet [Free Churches' Education Board]

FU   Folkuniversitetet [Folk University]

KFUK/M   KFUK-KFUM:s Studieförbund [National Educational Association for the YWCA and YMCA]

Mbsk   Medborgarskolan [Citizens' Educational Association]

NBV   Nykterhetsrörelsens Bildningsverksamhet [Educational Association of the Temperance Movement]

Sfr Studiefrämjandet [Study Promotion As-
      sociation]

SKS Sveriges Kyrkliga Studieförbund [Edu-
      cational Association of the Swedish
      Church]

SV Studieförbundet Vuxenskolan [Adult
      Schools Association]

TBV Tjänstemännens Bildningsverksamhet
      [Salaried Employees Educational Associa-
      tion]

Allan Sundqvist, chairman of the National Swedish
Federation of Adult Education Associations (SFHL),
points out that even though the associations differ with
regard to goals and priorities, they share certain principles:

> [T]hey enjoy the right and freedom to criticize
> and question ideas and value judgments no mat-
> ter what their source. If democracy is to be pre-
> served and developed, means must be put in hand
> for a free exchange of views based on respect for
> facts and an honest resolve to shed . . . light on
> the issues involved.
>
> Another goal that adult educators share in com-
> mon is to help people educate themselves as part
> of the lifelong learning process. For many, the
> study circle has become indissolubly wedded to
> their lifestyles, a natural part of the daily round.
> No other form of adult education has the mobility
> and the nearness to people that are necessary to
> meet these needs.[1]

These associations have a virtual monopoly on study
circle activity, yet the diversity of their "profiles" (or

ideological positions) and attendant study circle programs provides the public with a wide range of subject offerings.

The Worker's Educational Association (ABF), the largest study circle association, directs its educational activities, including study circles, to the blue-collar industrial unions, to Social Democratic party (SAP) members, and to the consumer cooperatives. It has forty-three affiliated organizations; publishes its own magazine, *Fonstret* (The Window); and takes positions on national educational and cultural policy and often on other public issues.

ABF study organizers are paid staff in all twenty-three hundred ABF local branch organizations (or "clubs"), and each local club conducts as few as ten and up to dozens of circles. Many ABF study circle participants have limited formal education, work in heavy industry, and have enormous loyalty to their study circles. One respondent, Irina Blid at Brunnsvik College, said her father, a factory shop steward, "had been a study circle leader for ABF for twenty-five years and never missed a session."

ABF study circles include those sponsored by SAP. Jan Ahltorp, the SAP official responsible for study circles and materials, reported that "all official SAP circles are conducted within ABF. . . . Since SAP has 1.2 million party members, there is a substantial base for support of the ABF study circles." He pointed out that any group of SAP local party members can start a study circle, usually affiliating with ABF to get the government subsidy.

Local ABF clubs plan their own study circle agendas, approve the leaders, order materials, and recruit members. Almost half of ABF circles are conducted exclusively for union, cooperative, or SAP members; others

are open to public participants. Since the government
offers substantial increased subsidies for study circles
on English, math, civics, the Swedish language for
immigrants, and other topics, half of the ABF study
circles qualify annually for these additional awards.

One third of the blue-collar union members participating in ABF's study circles do so in "workplace
circles," and most of the unions supplement government support to their circles with their own subsidies,
so the cost to the workers is minimal or nonexistent.
Many of the union study organizers are elected by their
fellow workers and trained by ABF in short courses
at the work site; these courses are often subsidized by
the employer as part of the collective bargaining agreement. Even so, only 15 percent of the trade union
members participate annually in the study circles,
which means that ABF study programs cannot be concentrated solely on trade union topics or political issues; they must be broad enough to attract the general
public or they lose the state subsidy.

KFUK/M, the National Educational Association for
the YWCA and YMCA, lies at the other end of the
spectrum from ABF as the smallest of the associations.
One of the first popular movements, with Swedish Y's
organized around the turn of the century, KFUK/M
has few full-time staff to conduct its five thousand
annual study circles. Although each of its twenty-four
local branches has its own study organizer, KFUK/M,
in contrast to ABF and some of the other larger associations, does not publish its own materials. Its materials
come from Brevskolan, the ABF printing house; from
the Swedish Educational Broadcasting Company (UR);
and from other outside sources.

"Because we are small," said Lena Samuelsson of
KFUK/M, "the Y's have attracted some of the smaller

political parties (e.g., the Christian Democratic party) unaffiliated with another national association, or we have organizations like the Boy Scouts that often produce their own materials. They join us so that their study circles can be reported through our national association to obtain the government subsidy." Samuelsson said KFUK/M "does not have an ideological profile, although some of the member organizations do."

KFUK/M's study circles mainly concentrate on cultural subjects, although recently it has begun to increase its study circle activities on topics such as international peace, the environment, and the future, some of which are eligible for government incentive subsidies.

Sfr, or Study Promotion Association, the second smallest national association, includes most of the leisure-time organizations as its affiliates and emphasizes environmental concerns, nature, animals, and natural phenomena. Sfr also conducts study circles on languages, handicrafts, and civics in efforts to attract nonmembers from the general public. It has no political ties. Even though it conducts only 5 percent of Sweden's study circles annually, it has its own publishing house for member organizations, with over two hundred titles to its credit.

Some 25 percent of the local Sfr study circles are conducted for members of affiliated organizations; 75 percent reach a public attracted by the subject matter, the materials, or simply good recruiting. Despite its size, Sfr has nineteen regional or district offices, one hundred local chapters, four hundred employees, and eight thousand study circle leaders who conduct fifteen thousand circles annually.

Recruitment and promotion are critical for the local association offices of all the national associations. Even

the Folk University, a university-affiliated association
with no members or member organizations and with
no political, religious, trade union, or other special
group identification, "has to print brochures announc-
ing its study circles and compete with the other associations for public participants," according to Anders
Höglund of the Extra-Mural Board of Stockholm University and a Folk University director. The Folk University is the fifth largest of the national associations
and, in Höglund's view, "the most independent because
of our university base." The Folk University tends to
focus its study circle programs on languages, followed
by art, other cultural subjects, and advanced studies
for professionals often led by university faculty.

Peter Engberg of SFHL told me that "the essence
of the study circles, the key to understanding the success of the circles in Sweden, is the link to the national
associations, not the small group methodology." There
is remarkable similarity in the way the ten associations
organize to carry out their study circle activities, even
though they differ enormously in size, resources, and
number of circles. The real differences, however,
come in the degree to which some of the associations
develop their own program initiatives and materials,
and recruit their own members to their circles (primarily
from the political parties and the trade unions),
while others such as the Folk University and the Y's
use materials from outside sources and primarily recruit study circle participants from the general public.
To maintain the government subsidies, however, all
the national associations try as much as possible to
attract a general public to their study circles. There
are just not enough "member circles" to gain the basic
grants.

The fundamental organizational pattern followed by

almost all the national associations includes full-time staff at three levels: national office, regional (or district) offices, and local, community-based offices. At each level there is an advisory board, which advises on the use of the government grants and the study circle programs.

By way of illustration, consider the largest and the smallest associations. ABF is a national bureaucracy rivaling most government agencies. It has, for example, ninety full-time staff in its Stockholm offices, 21 district offices, and 154 local offices covering the length and breadth of the country. ABF claims approximately one third (120,000) of all the study circles in Sweden, over 40 percent of all circle participants, and a government subsidy of SEK 120 million (Swedish kronors) annually ($15 million).

In contrast, KFUK/M has only a handful of staff in its national office in Stockholm, 9 district offices, and 24 local offices. KFUK/M accounts for only 1 percent of the nation's circles (5,000) and 2 percent of the participants. Even so, KFUK/M has roughly the same national-district-local office structure as the much larger ABF.

For all the national associations, both paid and voluntary staff function at all three organizational levels, carrying out such daily tasks as approving study plans, identifying circle leaders, determining materials, and providing logistical support for the local study organizers, along with training leaders, and evaluating and assessing study circle results.

But in a view unanimously endorsed by the interviewees, the success of the study circle *locally* hinges on the local study organizers at the community, factory, or town level. These organizers are paid staff, part time or full time, who are often elected by their peers. Working out of the national association's local office, a union hall, the factory floor, a community center, or even a private home, study organizers recruit circle members, help to develop study circle plans, identify and train leaders, obtain materials, and follow up on logistical matters.

The trade unions alone employ over sixty thousand study organizers, many carrying out study circle recruitment at the workplace with employer approval and on company time. These organizers are responsible for over 150,000 study circles annually for trade union members, almost one half of all the circles in the country.[2]

Government support for the national educational associations to carry out their study circle programs has assured Swedish adults broad opportunities to join circles of their choice. Government subsidies are substantial; study circles receive 80 to 90 percent of their costs from national, municipal, or county sources. These subsidies have survived changes in the Swedish government,[3] with the national government setting aside approximately SEK 900 million ($113 million) annually for study circle activities. The program is administered through the Adult Education Division of the Ministry of Education and Cultural Affairs (led by political appointees) and advised by the National Swedish Board of Education (subject matter specialists). In addition, SFHL links the ten national associations, providing a clearinghouse along with research functions.

The government's rules for study circles were changed in 1981 by the Liberal-Center-Moderate coalition. The new rules were designed to link the national associations' programs more directly with their members' interests in adult education, and to reduce undue paperwork, bureaucratic tendencies, and institutionalization. They were also designed to create more flexibility in study circle activities at the local level.

Specifically, the 1981 reforms simplified the subsidy rules and administrative procedures, giving the national associations increased freedom to adhere more closely to their respective profiles in their study circle programs. New "flat rate grants" (block grants) replaced the former grants for local study circle leaders and materials. Each association now receives a *basic grant* for all reported study circle hours up to a predetermined number of hours (approximately 70 percent of activities), and a variable but lower *per-hour grant* with no maximum ceiling for all other study circle hours. An association must vouch only for the study hours reported, regardless of costs, which thus gives it increased flexibility to use the government funds for its own program initiatives. Special supplemental or incentive study hour grants for the disabled, the rural dweller, and the aging are still available, along with the special grants for civic affairs, mathematics, and instruction in the Swedish language for immigrants.

The new rules also tightened eligibility requirements for subsidy: a study circle must have at least five and no more than twenty participants and must be in session for at least fifteen hours over a minimum of four weeks. These rules ensure that the circles will be small enough so all can participate, and that they will meet long enough sequentially to probe the materials in depth.

Since government grants for study circles are awarded for total study circle hours, national associations make their appeals for participants both to members and to the public. This makes for lively competition for participants, and the study organizers recruit by selling the attractiveness of their respective circles—the sponsor, the subject matter, the circle leader, the quality or point of view of the materials, the reputation of a particular organizer, a circle's longevity, and, not to be overlooked, the effectiveness of the association's publicity campaign.

The local campaign often includes direct mailings by the study organizers, advertisements in local newspapers, prominently displayed posters, presentations at meetings and public gatherings, pamphlets in supermarkets or on the shop floor, and, more often than not, door-to-door solicitation.

The intense competition for study circle recruits in local communities does not bother Sven-Eric Henricson of the National Swedish Board of Education, who observed:

> The public understands the "profiles" or position of each sponsoring national association, and some of the associations develop their own materials— e.g., on the environment, on nuclear questions. Each association has to organize locally, because people are recruited to study circles by their own interests. The public chooses. So there is strong competition for participants, and the public benefits by the wealth of subjects offered.

The system seems to work, with 2.9 million adult Swedes participating annually in study circles. Yet the substantial government subsidies and the resultant widespread proliferation of study circles has led to elaborate bureaucracies on the national and regional levels, and to spirited and intense competition for circle participants on the local level. Overlapping programs in a community or town have often been the norm, not the exception, but as Leif Klint of TBV, the Salaried Employees Educational Association, put it:

The networks are there and are used, and the public benefits. The best circles are those that pursue studies based on the ongoing interests of their circle members. This keeps them together and keeps them coming back. If they deviate from the participants' interests, the circles fail. But it is always a "hard sell" by the study organizers. So, in order to keep a circle going, they never end without asking, "What do we do next?"

The importance of the paid study organizers in this local competitive setting was underlined in an example offered by Leif Pettersson, ombudsman for the Swedish Confederation of Trade Unions (LO). Pettersson mentioned Boden, a town in the north of Sweden, where "there are 294 union members, almost all in study circles. . . . This union helps to subsidize the circles, and many take place in the work sites. . . . The study organizers go out and talk to the people, but in a nearby town, Udval, the local hospital decided to promote and conduct study circles on its own, but no one came. It comes back to organizing and having a catalyst."

There is also a dichotomy between the extensive bureaucracy needed to conduct the circles and the regulations that have always come with government subsidies on the one hand, and the much-advertised, "free-wheeling nature" of some of the national educational associations as "popular movements" on the other. By definition, the associations should be antithetical to bureaucratic practice, but advocates argue that the system has to be organized both to hold the associations accountable for the public funding and to ensure diverse opportunities for adults interested in furthering their education through the study circles.

One interviewee suggested that this very diversity

has caused critics to question whether it is "necessary
and practical . . . to have so many associations competing, for example, in the same city, town, or region."
The trick for this respondent was "to maintain the
vitality and creativity of the associations while recog-
nizing the necessity of having cumbersome bureaucratic structures to carry out the mission."

Nevertheless, in spite of the competition, all ten
national associations seem to be thriving and receiving
top government subsidies, and the ultimate beneficiary, the Swedish adult public, continues to respond
by participating annually in large numbers in study
circles of their own choosing.

3

· ·

Pedagogy and Content

Peter Engberg and several other respondents observed that the key to understanding the success of the Swedish study circles lies in the ten national associations and their ability to obtain subsidies and promote the local circles. Yet the Swedes devote substantial research and writing to understanding *how* the study circles work—"the pedagogy of the study circle," as they call it. They are not overly concerned with why adults participate, a preoccupation of adult educators in the United States, but they are deeply concerned with getting the results of their research back to the field.

Contrary to adult education theory in several European countries and in the United States, where many educators prefer to call their field *andragogy*, making a distinction between a science of teaching children and one of teaching adults, the Swedes prefer to talk about *pedagogy*, the teaching-learning format in which all participants learn, regardless of age.

By pedagogy, the Swedes mean simply how adults learn to work in small groups—the dynamics of the study circle format as an adult learning experience, given the history and philosophical principles underlying the study circle concept in Sweden. "The study circle is a special form of small group study," writes Norman Kurland of the New York State Study Circle Consortium, adding that, as it is practiced in Sweden, "it is a highly structured, informal system of popular adult education."[1]

One guiding principle is that study circles can be held in factories, community centers, libraries, union halls, corporate board rooms, churches—almost anywhere adults with similar educational interests can gather. Another principle is that adults who choose to participate in the study circles—regardless of sponsor, site, or subject matter—tend to share a set of common understandings about the theory and practice of study circles and popular (adult) education.

The Swedes, for example, stress the "free and voluntary" nature of study circles, a phrase that appears in all the literature and means that participants are free to choose a circle and come to this form of adult education voluntarily. There is no formal credit involved; the study circle is not a classroom. There are no prerequisites. Instead of employing a teacher or other content specialist, study circles examine a topic in depth through give-and-take discussion and, in the process, provide participants with practical experience in group cooperation. Respondents quickly pointed out that participants take great pride in the study circle's democratic atmosphere, which encourages cooperation in learning by capitalizing on the collective experience of the group.

Henry Blid of Brunnsvik College, a circle leader and professor of adult education, writes about what study circles should be. He describes adult education as a living, activist process that relates knowledge to action and social change, to development and creativity, and to social intercourse and collective development. Such education provides knowledge that is intelligible to adult learners, whatever their educational backgrounds, and teaches adults to be analytical and critical of existing practice, and to challenge myths and prejudices wherever found. Blid's pedagogical principles for study circles include

> *Equality and democracy among circle participants,* with all members acting at one time as both teachers and students, and with reliance on dialogue and conversation rather than on lectures, outside experts, or formal presentations (except at the direction of the circle).

> *Liberation of members' inherent capabilities and innate resources,* empowering them to act, and to influence and be influenced by social reality.

> *Cooperation and companionship,* with members working together toward agreed-upon ends, finding "common ground" in their relationships and ideas.

> *Study and liberty, and member self-determination* of formats and direction, based upon their needs and wishes, and on the objectives of the sponsoring association.

> *Continuity and planning,* meaning enough time for conversations that overcome "onesidedness," withdrawal of individuals, and undue pushing of one's point of view, along with emphasis on creating interest in further study after the circle ends. This also means planning by the members themselves, who have the ability to change plans as the need arises.

Study circles differ from open-ended discussion groups and radio/TV "listening groups," which often do not have systematic study as their goal.

Active member participation to encourage cooperation, joint responsibility, and conversation, without which there is no study circle.

As Blid points out, "the members' active contribution is the cornerstone on which are built not only study circles but also the far more important democracy. . . . People learn best when they are active." With groups that are too small, it is difficult to maintain conversation; with larger groups, few participate, so the study circles are officially charged with having a lower (five) and upper (twenty) limit.

Use of printed study materials, from pamphlets, journal extracts, and newspaper articles to scientific texts (used in more advanced circles). Printed matter is always used to supplement circle conversations.[2]

Blid's statement encompasses the study circle pedagogy—simple, straightforward, learner-centered and democratic, and voluntary. For the 2.9 million Swedes who participate annually, there seems to be universal acceptance of these principles.

The Swedes have substantial data on who participates in the 325,000 study circles conducted annually, since all circle leaders have to provide full reports on the demographics of their participants to be eligible for government subsidies. The national associations with registered members (trade unions, political parties, temperance groups, and church organizations) conduct both member circles, attended exclusively by their members, and general circles for the walk-in public.

The study circles attract a spectrum of Swedish society, and no segment is overlooked—from the recent immigrants from Southeast Asia, Chile, or Finland to the scientific professionals who attend the Folk University's circles on advanced scientific and technological developments. Further, if the government believes a designated population, such as the handicapped or rural dwellers, has limited access to adult education, it creates a special supplemental grant category to spur study circle development in this area. This results in the priority circles, which reach special target populations or concentrate on special subjects such as civic affairs. By providing the national associations with such financial incentives, the government encourages them to break through traditional middle-class barriers so prevalent in adult education in advanced nations, and to give those outside mainstream adult education programs the opportunity to participate.

Lena Samuelsson of the KFUK/M provided an example of this point. A sizable Vietnamese immigrant population in Nyköping, just south of Stockholm, met in study circles with young Swedes under the auspices of KFUK/M, which received supplementary state funding for the project. They videotaped their discussions, and the edited tape became the basis for a popular television documentary used in other study circles throughout the country.

Even with the subsidies as incentives, a report by the National Swedish Board of Education in 1983 indicates that there is still a lot to do:

> If anything, generational inequalities are greater than ever. . . . It is still sex, family tradition, social status, ethnic background, geographical accessibility and personal finances that decide

whether there can be any question of an individual taking part in adult education, and, if so,
what type of studies.

The report goes on to note that "those who have had
the least education appear to stay put on their side of
the educational gap. . . . There are psychological impediments which have to be overcome, and positive
attitudes to education will have to be inculcated among
the people belonging to priority groups."[3]
    Each national association has a reputation for reach-
ing beyond the already educated. ABF, for example,
because of its working-class orientation and SAP blue-
collar union affiliations, has deliberately tried to attract
the undereducated, as well as immigrants, who seem
to receive the attention of all the national associations.
In contrast, when asked about reaching out to undereducated adults, Leif Kindblom, director of the Sfr,
replied that

> Sfr is not indifferent to the undereducated but
> attempts to spread out to many people, in con-
> trast to ABF's focus on trade union members. We
> reach many young people who are attracted by
> our "antibureaucratic profile" and our concern
> with the environment and our ability to move fast
> to catch fast-developing issues.

Government reports indicate that approximately
half of the study circle participants are women. They
tend to dominate in cultural subjects but participate
equally with men in circles on language and civic affairs. Women are dramatically underrepresented,
however, in the newer circles dealing with computer
science issues and data processing. Nevertheless, more
and more women are joining circles at the workplace,

once a male province, as women rise to positions of leadership in the trade unions and the companies. Finally, study circle participation greatly depends on the resources and enthusiasm of the local study organizers, and on the forcefulness of national association officials who want to promote a specific course of study. For example, in one study that examined study organizers' practices in Mora, a small town 150 miles northwest of Stockholm, researchers asked local study association officials (seven of the ten national associations had branch offices here) what they thought was the primary role of their study circles. The branch officials responded as follows:

ABF: The ABF task is providing an opportunity to study for those who, earlier in their lives, had unequal study opportunities.

SV: The Mora branch office should be a good complement to the other study organizations.

Mbsk: (affiliated with the Conservative party): We should work for all-around education concerning current affairs as well as culture.

TBV: Although trade union education should be our main purpose, the members do not think that trade union education is fun. So it is our task to try and make people meet and to have a good time together.

NBV: Member training is important, along with support of association studies and cultural activities.

SKS: We provide positive leisure-time activities offering people many alternatives.

Sfr: We train people who never had received
much formal education.[4]

The rationales differed remarkably, based on the interest of the national association, but all associations
seemed successful in promoting and recruiting participants for their circles in this small town.

Study circle participants develop their knowledge
and judgments by interacting with circle members,
the leader, and the study materials. The leader is also
a participant and assists by providing information, by
making sure that choices and problem-solving ap-
proaches are clear, and by ensuring that everyone
takes part: "All of the members of the study circle
must be teachers and students in relation to one
another. Each member is responsible for others and
not only for himself."[5]

Study circle leaders can be local officials, organizational members, or just public-minded citizens. Many
natural leaders emerge from the study circle participants themselves. But wherever the leader comes
from, a study circle can elect to choose its own, from
within the group or outside, subject to the approval
of the sponsoring association (e.g., a study circle on
environmental pollution would probably not have a representative of the polluting firm as the circle leader).
Thus, the study circle members have the right to accept
or reject the designated circle leader: "The supreme
authority rests with the circle members," as one respondent put it.

There are no formal requirements for study circle
leaders, except that they must be familiar with the
subject matter and be comfortable with the aims of
popular education. According to Blid, "the best study
circle leaders are generally those who possess the same

interests and backgrounds as the study circle members themselves."[6]

Leadership training, however, is rarely left to chance. All leaders receive some form of training, usually under the auspices of the sponsoring national association. The trade unions, for example, like the Swedish Confederation of Trade Unions (LO) and the Central Organization of Salaried Employees (TCO), like to train their own study circle leaders and organizers, using trade union materials and conducting most of the training in local union offices. Training usually combines instruction and practical experience, and occasionally uses role playing to familiarize leaders with study circle methodology and the administrative chores they must carry out. Thus, the Adult Schools Association (SV), related to the Liberal party, holds six hundred courses for its study circle leaders annually, mostly in collaboration with the folk high schools. The training includes group psychology, a survey of popular adult education in Sweden, and study circle teaching methods. SV also trains leaders in specific subject matter and offers special training for circles for the handicapped.

Study circle leaders are considered key to the circles' effectiveness. They are not teachers in the traditional, classroom sense; as members of the study circle who are approved or elected by the other members, they guide but do not direct the circle. Their main task is to organize the circle's study plan based on the decisions of the members. They are then to monitor the circle's progress according to its plan and to promote a positive, cooperative atmosphere or social climate by being a good listener, getting to know the members, encouraging member initiative and participation, and gaining the members' confidence. They are also resource people in organizing the study circle. However, they play down any role as expert or subject matter specialist.

"Good leaders," according to *The Study Associations in Sweden*, the pamphlet of the National Swedish Federation of Adult Education Associations (SFHL), "take responsibility for their circles and for their members' learning; they inspire member self-confidence by bringing them into the group; they create a positive atmosphere; they tone down their own role; they know when to encourage and when to restrain a member; and they keep the circle activities varied and moving."[7] A number of respondents in this study admitted that knowledge of the subject matter can be important, but they tended to stress even more leader knowledge of group dynamics and the social-psychological aspects of group work.

As noted earlier, one of the most attractive features of the study circle is that it can be organized anywhere a small group can meet, unrestricted by the needs of a lecture hall or large auditorium, complicated audiovisual and public address systems, and maintenance costs. As the Swedes lovingly point out, the original study circles at the turn of the century started in homes, farmhouses, church meeting rooms, and union halls. Trade unions, for instance, use their union halls or corporate facilities, and in larger cities there are special buildings designed exclusively for study circle activity, usually encompassing district and local offices.

Libraries, public schools, and churches have always been popular sites for study circles, especially in smaller towns with few public meeting facilities. I personally witnessed several study circles in such settings as a folk high school in Ludvika, a municipal building in Stockholm, and a "people's park" (an amusement-education center, which is usually owned jointly by the trade unions and the municipality) in Malmö. Private homes are discouraged, however, because of the potential distractions. Corporations encourage study circles for employees. The 1975 "Annual Educational Leave Act" gave employees the right to time off for continuing education, and many large companies, as part of the union contract, offer employees time off during work hours to pursue study circle work. Shop stewards and plant organizers, by law, can organize study circles at the work site, and some of these circles include training for the elected study circle organizers who establish in-plant circles for union members. Also, the 1977 "Co-Determination Act" gave employees in companies employing twenty-five or more persons the option to appoint two board members, who are then trained in study circle courses which can take place in the company.[8]

Sweden's early twentieth-century study circles were developed to further the objectives of the popular movements. Thus, the temperance and free church movements taught sobriety, discipline, and hard work. The blue-collar, industrial unions and the Social Democratic party taught class struggle, organizing, and social change. The KFUK/M (the Y's) emphasized family values. All the popular movements envisioned their study circles contributing to the general uplifting of educational standards among their adult constituents and, in the process, developing untapped local and national leadership.

But the early study circles had few written materials to draw upon, and their content emerged from the conditions and daily lives of the participants. In con-

trast, today's ten national associations, along with their
publishing houses, generate substantial study circle
publications, usually along the lines of their ideological
bent or profile. Thus, we find the ABF materials stress-
ing trade union affairs, labor legislation, leadership
skills, industrial democracy, trade union skills, labor
history, and labor-management relations. The SAP circles tend to focus on campaign issues, party organizing
and recruitment, and internal party matters. KFUK/M
emphasizes music, Bible studies, social affairs, and international understanding in keeping with the mission
of the Y movement. Sfr, because of its appeal to youth
and environmental groups, develops materials about
nature, the environment, energy, conservation, and
the planet Earth.

Outside of their profiles, all ten national associations
go beyond their organizational concerns to conduct circles on more general, cultural content—languages, history, literature, arts, theater—to attract the general
public. If an adult Swede has an interest in studying
something, either there will be an existing study circle
to join sponsored by one of the associations, or a new
circle can be formed with a minimum of five members
and it can link up with an association to obtain the
subsidy. As one acquaintance said, "I wanted to learn
Dutch, so I found five others who were also interested,
we got the ABF sponsorship, and I led the circle."

Statistically, three-fourths of the study circle hours
are devoted to general cultural subjects and civic affairs; the remaining time is spent on an organizational
interest of the national associations. Trade union and
political party officials I interviewed reported increased study circle discussion in the 1980s on civics
and public issues. The government undoubtedly spurred
this interest in public affairs when it encouraged study

circles to discuss the nuclear power alternatives in
1979 prior to the 1980 referendum on the issue (see
chap. 4); and, once again, the government offers incentive grants for circles on civic affairs. Nevertheless,
Patrick Breslin of the ABF observed that

> demographic changes have affected what partic-
> ipants study—the older generation tended
> toward study circles on trade union or party
> affairs, whereas younger people, no longer class
> loyal or trade union-oriented, are looking to
> circles for knowledge and skills, such as computer
> studies, to obtain jobs. I think it is the same way
> in your country.

Breslin and others also noted that many study circle
members, after being involved initially in cultural activities and issues of similar content, tended to take
on more political and social issues in their circles the
longer they stayed together. This "consciousness-
raising" role of the study circle was corroborated by
a research study carried out by Gosta Vestlund, former
Ministry of Education official. Vestlund examined
three suburban communities near Stockholm and reported that one-third of the participants in circles on
cultural-civic affairs tended to go on to become active
in community and political life, often for the first time.[9]
    In another study cited by Breslin, the LO and the
ABF attempted to start some study circles in a local
hospital several years ago. Over 30 percent of the hospital workers participated, with three-fourths demand-
ing to study languages (English and French), ceramics,
painting, and other cultural subjects; only a fourth
wanted to talk about trade union issues, political affairs, or public issues. Four years after they began,
the same study circles reported that the percentage

wanting to discuss union or party affairs—organizing, work rights, and health and safety—had risen to 50 percent.

Leif Klint of TBV offered a rationale for this behavior: "Many new circle participants start with non-threatening subjects like painting and handicrafts, which bring them in. But being in a circle creates a local network, and the participants, if they stay together, often go on to more political subjects." Many labor union and political party officials I spoke to echoed Klint's point: study circles devoted to civic affairs have increased dramatically over the last few years.

The ten national associations publish and promote their own literature or recommend for their study circles print and audiovisual materials that reflect their profile. Brevskolan, for example, provides ABF with 65 percent of its study circle materials. The booklets I reviewed, all in English, appeared highly readable and amply illustrated, with plentiful photos and drawings along with well-stated discussion questions. Some of the topics were "Your Own Trade Union," "Your Rights at Work," "Working Environment and Participation in Joint Decision-Making," "From Consultation to Co-Determination," "Industrialization and Computerization," and "Chemical Hazards to Health."

Occasionally, a publishing house like Brevskolan will generate study circle materials designed to initiate circle activity. Ulf-Göran Widqvist of Brevskolan said that as many as one-third of Brevskolan's titles were initiated by staff and funded by Brevskolan, with solid promotion at the local level. "Brevskolan," said Widqvist, "is heavily dependent on ABF's study circle activities and attempts to select topics for study and discussion that local study organizers will support."

During election campaigns, both Brevskolan and ABF strongly support the LO and SAP's political position in local, regional, and national contests. On the other hand, TBV, listening to Leif Klint, knows that only 15 percent of its white-collar and civil servant union affiliates participate in study circles, so it deliberately avoids concentrating on union topics in order to attract the broadest possible public to its circles.

In another example, the Folk University recently had to create its own publishing arm to produce teaching materials for the association's university-related circles, since general materials that are suitable for their sponsored circles were hard to come by. The Folk University's publications range from literacy materials for immigrants and works on the Third World to university-level, professionally oriented texts for circles on understanding science, data-processing, economics, and the law.

Study circles, regardless of sponsorship, are free to develop materials locally, and these are often brought in by the circle members. (According to Jan Ahltorp, "91 percent of our SAP circles use local materials.") Each association, however, differs in the degree to which it uses and encourages locally generated materials. The SFHL reported on the study carried out in Mora, a town of seventeen thousand: with seven of the national associations actively promoting and conducting study circles, only one, SV, encouraged development of local materials and local study plans; the other study circles ordered materials from the national associations.[10]

Other national organizations providing materials for the study circles are Liber Hermods, which publishes correspondence study materials such as language instruction or public issue topics often used in study

circles, including company-sponsored circles; and the
Swedish Broadcasting Corporation, which relates its
radio and television programs to the circles.

The Swedes have used radio programs in their study
circles for some time, but they have only recently been
experimenting with television programming and local
circles. Several respondents mentioned the beginning
of a cable TV industry in Sweden, especially in the
south, and thought cable TV held strong potential for
the study circle programs.

The Swedish Broadcasting Corporation (SR) includes Swedish Radio (AB), which in turn has responsibility for the two Swedish television channels, the
Swedish Local Radio Company, and the Swedish Educational Broadcasting Company (UR). The government heavily subsidizes and regulates radio and television in Sweden, and it names the SR board, 60 percent
of whose members represent the ten national educational associations, 20 percent come from industry and
commerce, and 20 percent come from the press.
Whereas Swedish television, with two major channels,
is highly centralized, Swedish radio is decentralized
with emphasis on regional programs. Especially in language studies, Swedish radio, with twenty-four local
stations, is tied in closely with the study circles. Both
television and radio are linked under the same management in many parts of the country, with television
rapidly establishing regional production centers in a
first step toward decentralization of the broadcasting
system.

Most of the links between the media and the study
circles are effected by UR, which is wholly government
supported but has its own board. UR broadcasts over
both radio and television, has an extensive adult edu-

cation program, and often produces booklets, brochures, and discussion guides to accompany its broadcasts.

Collaboration between the media and the study circles comes about in two ways: the national associations can initiate their own radio-TV programs for their sponsored circles, or UR develops programs on topics such as language instruction or civic affairs and then promotes them to the study circles through their respective national associations. One UR spokesperson, Gunilla Sterner-Kumm, said that "language instruction on TV mushroomed in the early 1970s when we started developing special programs for the study circles." She observed that UR broadcasts over five hundred hours of television annually, seven hundred hours of national radio, and one hundred hours of local radio programming.

Additionally, each year UR produces ninety hours of new television programs, all with government underwriting, and most are available for local study circle use. Sterner-Kumm is convinced that as television expands to its regional production centers, and as cable TV becomes more generally available, UR will develop an increasing range of programs on television for the circles, with the national associations increasingly coming to UR for tailored programs to be used in their study circles.

All respondents discussing the use of media, however, stressed television and radio as supplemental to the study circles' primary focus—dialogue and conversation among the members—and were fearful of the media's intrusion on the study circle small-group process. But there seemed to be strong interest in finding ways to relate television and radio to study circle work while maintaining the integrity of the study circles' principles and pedagogy.

The use of the media is not the only issue that brings
out the tensions between the predetermined format and
content of study circles and the free and voluntary
nature inherent in their pedagogy. Several respondents pointed out the distinction between adult education on the one hand, as it is practiced in the study
circles with no preconceived end results but with a
concentration on individual growth, and public policy
or political education on the other hand, which primarily entails information campaigns with predetermined
points of view and predictable outcomes. Almost all
political information campaigns are directed toward
members of organizations affiliated with a national association, especially the trade unions and the political
parties. Often a study circle may set out to participate
in an information campaign, however, and wind up
with no consensus as a result of the intense discussion—to the chagrin of the sponsoring association.

Even though study circle organizers submit their
plans to the branch offices of the national organizations
and these plans are funneled up through channels, the
national associations have no systematic mechanism
for reporting the outcomes of study circles, outside of
demographic data and circle content. LO's Leif
Pettersson had a succinct comment when asked about
communicating the substantive results of the study
circles, particularly those that dealt with civic affairs
and public issue discussion: "People who come to the
circles are not interested in collective outcomes. There
is no feedback mechanism as most circle members are
in the circle for the sake of learning. It's what they
want to do—the motivation is intrinsic."

Pettersson's view that what happens in the study
circle is the most important outcome is shared by the
other respondents. Several went further to point out

that the study circle has been an ideal educational format for Sweden and has contributed substantially to the development of the nation's social democratic character. And with their simple and straightforward egalitarianism, study circles have enabled citizens to acquire both the knowledge and the skills necessary for active participation in civic life. Since many of the country's leaders have emerged from the study circle movement, they are themselves sensitive to the importance of the study circles as vehicles for citizens to understand public life and issues and to enhance individual self-esteem and personal growth. And they admit to being more concerned than ever before with continuing to encourage the study circles, through the national associations, to take on civic affairs and important issues facing the Swedish public.

4

· ·

Public Issue Campaigns

Swedish study circles were founded primarily to provide workers, the undereducated, and the disenfranchised with a forum for understanding and participating in public life. All the national associations, to one degree or another, engage their study circles in civic affairs or some form of public issue discussion. In a 1976 study of twenty representatives from the national associations, for example, officials from eight of the associations believed their organizations will be increasingly concerned with public issue discussion. "It may even develop," the report states, "into the most important part of the study organizations' entire activity." The report concludes:

> society is becoming more and more complex and
> in such a society the individual shows an increas-
> ing need for thorough explanation of social
> problems in order to be able to follow social
> developments. The importance of strengthening
> democracy in this way is often mentioned.[1]

But some of the respondents I interviewed felt the national associations had to be reminded on occasion of the importance of public policy discussion to public life and of how far some of the associations may have come from their roots. Indeed, several respondents observed that Sweden could have gone through a violent revolution at the turn of the century if education and culture had not been spread to ordinary people through the study circles. Peter Engberg noted that "the temperance movement and the labor movement wanted their own form of adult education because of their disappointment with the formal educational system, and found it in the study circles." The early circles, said Engberg, "focused on 'stomach issues'—basic economies—and on educating workers to understand the political structure so they could more effectively participate in civic life."

Engberg's observation was reinforced by television commentator Lars Ulvenstam, who reflected that "traditionally, the Social Democratic party and the trade unions built their popular bases by creating an informed public, by using study circles." But over the last several decades, he continued, "the success of the Swedish formal educational system has led more adults into cultural pursuits, not issue discussion, and people have lost their ideological orientation and their intensity for civic affairs."

Thus, study circles in Sweden today are *not* organized exclusively for public issue discussion, even though civics and political issues can occupy up to a third of the circles annually. And although the supplemental grants for civic affairs and for what the Swedes call national issue campaigns stimulate circle activity in these areas, the government officials I spoke to went out of their way to stress the government's neutrality in such programs.

Agneta Charpentier, the Ministry of Education official responsible for government grants to the national associations, emphasized that study circle content "is not initiated by the state and is not organized from the top." She went on to add that study circles "are 'free and voluntary,' and it is up to the circle if they want to discuss public issues. We really don't want them talking too much about public issues—that's not their purpose."

Charpentier observed that the strength of the Swedish study circle movement is that "it works"— adults attend regularly in growing numbers to continue their education. But, she added, "study circle members do not directly influence public policy. They discuss what they want, but moving them to action is another question, and the state should never use them in this way for its own purposes."

Charpentier stressed that there have been occasional debates in Parliament on moving the study circles more into public issue discussion ("the mechanism is there and the temptation is strong"), but the national associations themselves have fought it. Moreover, there is power in funding, and on those occasions when the government wanted a national issue campaign, the provision of additional subsidies as incentives has succeeded in bringing all the national associations into the program. But Charpentier is herself uneasy with the use of government funding in this manner, since "it takes away something from the circles' voluntary nature. . . . At least in the national issue campaigns," she said, "we stress the need for objectivity and balance, not propaganda, but it can become difficult to regulate."

Sven-Eric Henricson of the National Swedish Board of Education takes an even more extreme position. He doesn't believe in using study circles in any national issue campaign: "They are not instruments of government and the government should not interfere." Thus, the Swedes have evolved this magnificent and expansive adult education network, including adult civic education, and are willing in practice to accept government subsidies for priority circles on civic affairs and public issue discussion. Yet, they remain apprehensive about the government exploiting the study circles for its own purposes.

When the government does decide to conduct a national issue campaign, however, each national association tends to bring its own point of view or ideological stance to the issue. Hence, the balance or objectivity Charpentier and Henricson are seeking comes from the range of viewpoints represented by the national associations and from the freedom all Swedish adults have to choose which circle they want to join locally. Charpentier underlined this point:

> Suppose I am interested in peace questions; then I would go to ABF as they have some of the best materials on the issue. For the environment, I might go to Sfr or one of the other associations stressing this issue. But I'm free to choose, and it is up to the associations what they concentrate on.

Despite official reluctance to use study circles for government purposes, it was natural for the Swedish government, with its power to create substantial subsidies, to turn to the study circle network for nationwide debate when faced with a pressing national issue. "What do the people think about the issue after discussing it fully?" asked one respondent. "That's what we are seeking in these national issue campaigns."

Government subsidies were used for the first time to promote a nationwide dialogue in 1955 when the

Social Democratic government wanted the country to switch from left- to right-hand driving (Sweden has always been enamored of English customs). The results of this effort, however, were unexpected. The government encouraged a national "information campaign," with its own point of view on the issue decidedly for the change. According to Anders Clasen, director of the Swedish Institute, "the government made no attempt to present alternative arguments—merely why it was important to make the change. It was purely an information campaign."

The referendum that followed the national discussions showed the Swedish public to be unwilling to change, with a 90 percent majority rejecting the government's initiative. The public's arguments ranged from the effect of the change on older people and the fear of injuries, to a basic apprehension about change itself. In short, the public did not accept the government's arguments, and the campaign backfired.

The "popular will" is often unpredictable, usually conservative, and may well be contrary to a party's policies, as happened in 1955. The upshot of that endeavor was that the government backed away from the change, but in 1967, by legislative decree, it ordered the country to stop driving for one hour, and Swedes simply moved their cars to the right lane without protest. Henricson believes the change in driving habit, when it finally came, was made easier because of the 1955 study circle debates and the continuing interest over the next twelve years in periodically readdressing the issue.

Widqvist of Brevskolan believes another national campaign, initiated by the government in 1958, helped sensitize and successfully prepare the country to replace the former "Old Age Fund" system with a new national general pension system based on the average of a worker's fifteen best years. According to Henricson:

> The Social Democrats won that one because the Liberals were split on the issue, and the right took an extreme position that the government should get out of the pension business altogether—people should have their own pension plans. The study circles helped to clarify the public's choices. . . . The public in a democratic society is always more receptive to a presentation of alternative choices than to a one-dimensional, government-sponsored information campaign.

Both the government and the national associations applied this lesson successfully in the national nuclear issue campaign of 1979. The following account illustrates how an objective national issue debate with spirited citizen involvement can affect national policy.

In 1976 the Liberal party, in coalition with the Center and Conservative (moderate) parties, took over the Swedish government—the first time the Social Democratic party was out of power since 1932. The nation's development of nuclear power was in full swing, but after the Three Mile Island disaster in Harrisburg, Pennsylvania, in 1978, Swedish public pressure intensified to end government support for building and licensing nuclear power plants.

The nation was split. The Center and Communist parties (an unusual alliance for Sweden) wanted to discontinue nuclear development; the Social Democrats and the Liberals (atypically on the same side of an issue, as several respondents noted) wanted to develop nuclear power slowly, then phase out new development so as to maintain jobs and energy independence; and the Conservatives opted for a "full speed ahead" policy.

Acknowledging these different positions, the Liberal government provided a series of study circle incentive grants to the national associations for a national issue campaign to begin on the question in September 1979. Since the issue would be presented to the voters in a binding referendum the following March, the study circle debates were to enable the citizenry to discuss the choices on the nuclear issue prior to the referendum. The ABF, the blue-collar unions under the LO, and the SAP opposed the national refendum, favoring instead increased public information on the issue. Once the national issue campaign was launched, however, these organizations encouraged their members to form study circles on the issue.

In fact, each national association joined the debate, publicizing the nuclear issue campaign heavily. Most weighed in with their own points of view, publishing their own materials, holding training programs for their study organizers, and encouraging active recruitment of the public. The trade unions, political parties, churches, and other member-affiliated organizations promoted the debate extensively among their constituents, adding the nuclear issue to their regular schedule of circle programs. Local study organizers became the ultimate arbiters for whose material would be used. Since study organizers are employed by the national associations, those associations with a predetermined position on the nuclear issue tended to discourage circles not in accord with their point of view. The citizens, as usual, were free to choose the circle that matched their interests.

On the other hand, some national associations such as the Folk University and KFUK/M did not take a position on the nuclear issue but encouraged their study circles to use materials reflecting the spectrum of viewpoints, including television and radio programs. The result, according to Eddie Levin of the Swedish Educational Broadcasting Company, was some confusion on the part of local circle participants:

> We produced six or seven programs on the nuclear issue on our own, and we had to compete with the associations in a mad scramble as each tried to get its own materials into the circles. There was too much information for the campaign, an overload, a saturation, and I believe many circle participants voted more from what they heard from others than from the circle discussions.

In an example of how materials can be generated almost overnight for study circle use, the Swedish Council for Planning and Coordination of Research, a quasi-governmental body, undertook a major publication campaign of its own on the nuclear issue, publishing a series of eleven booklets under the title *The Kalla* [source] *Series*. The booklets covered all aspects of the nuclear power debate, and each contained a dialogue between two individuals of contrasting views on the topic. The concept, according to Dyring and Vedin, the authors of the *Kalla Series* report, was called "scientific mediation," as a third author, a "mediator," commented on the debate presentations and clarified the public's choices. The low-priced booklets sold rapidly, with a reported 150,000 copies distributed in a few weeks. They were apparently well received and were used extensively in the study circle discussions.[2]

Peter Engberg called the nuclear debate "a true national discourse," with many of the 17,378 circles that addressed the issue using materials like the *Kalla Series*, which reflected a diversity of viewpoints. "It wasn't propaganda," said Engberg, "but a solid adult education program for an independent-minded public." Over 150,500 Swedes participated in the 1979 circle discussions.

The results of the March 1980 referendum were mixed. With three clear "lines" or positions on the ballot, the results were as follows: "Proceed with full development," 28 percent; "Develop nuclear power slowly, stop by 2010," 37 percent; and "Discontinue building nuclear plants," 35 percent.

There was similarly no consensus among the respondents in the present study on the significance of these results. Olle Edelholm of the Liberal party-affiliated Vuxenskolan (SV) and secretary-general of the Nordic Association of Adult Education said, "Without the national debate, we would have proceeded full speed ahead on nuclear development; it brought out the public to the referendum, many of whom might otherwise have stayed home." Widqvist concluded that "no one was happy with the results, but if we hadn't had the circles, Line 3 ["Discontinue development"], which we opposed, would clearly have won." SAP's Jan Ahltorp thought the results inconclusive and the effect of the study circle discussions "minimal." So there were even conflicting views about what the public would have done had the national study circle debate not taken place. But it did, and the public obviously responded through circle participation.

In some other outcomes of the referendum, Ahltorp observed that a surprisingly high 20 percent of the trade unionists, in spite of union leadership urging the nation to "go slow on development to maintain jobs," actually voted to stop development. Another association leader, Sfr's Leif Kindblom, said that even though his association did not take a position on the issue, "the majority of our members voted to stop development; we had a lot of study circle activity before the vote." Patrick Breslin said the ABF presented materials on all three positions, but "I don't know if they had any effect." And Anders Höglund, associated with the Folk University, thought "the debate helped to change the public's mind about nuclear power through the opportunity to debate the issue." Thus, most respondents in this study readily admitted that the referendum was undoubtedly informed by the preceding nationwide discussion and simply reflected the public's lack of consensus about nuclear power.

One unanticipated result of the nuclear debate and referendum was that the publicity surrounding the program brought out a lot of new study circle participants, and according to Agneta Charpentier, there is some evidence that "many of the circle participants, because of being engaged in the circle discussions, went on to become more interested in political matters."

Following the success of the national issue campaign in 1979–80, the new Social Democratic government (having regained power in 1982) sponsored another national campaign in 1982–83 on "Computer Power in Society." Again, the offer of substantial supplemental subsidies to the national associations for study circles on the issue brought about extensive circle discussions, resulting in a wealth of publications, including a new *Kalla Series*. The circles considered such issues as "The Computer: Master or Servant?" "Does the Computer Take Away Jobs?" and "Does Widespread Computer Power Lead to New Life Patterns?" Obviously, the debate over the influence of the computer on Swedish life was not as volatile an issue as the nuclear power question, but the public again joined study circles to discuss the topic, and the government has laid plans for further national issue campaigns on technology, nature, water use, and future studies.

Each of the ten national associations joined in the nuclear debate and again in the computer power debate in concerted nationwide discussions at the local level through the study circles. Each received substantial subsidies for engaging their study circles in the discussions. A few, however, like ABF because of its long-standing identification with SAP and LO, and TBV, which reaches white-collar union workers, address public issues of deep interest to their members regularly. The key to the success of these association-sponsored issue education campaigns seems to lie with the timeliness of the issue, the quality of the materials, the concern of the membership, and the aggressiveness and commitment of local study organizers.

For example, the interrelationship among ABF, LO, SAP, and KF (the Swedish Cooperative organization) along with Brevskolan is complex when it comes to issue discussion or study circles on civic affairs. Most ABF-sponsored circles are conducted in cooperation with LO and its member unions, with SAP officials and party members, and with members of KF. Brevskolan provides most of the publications for the circles, but each of these mass organizations has its own publishing capability. Each can and does initiate its own study circles. Interlocking issues committees made up of officials from each organization help coordinate the circles' activities on civic affairs and are reflected in similarly organized committees at the district and local levels.

One intriguing idea that came out of SAP and has been in operation for the past ten years is called *Idéforums* (issues forums), designed to meet annually after the Party Congress in September to address such issues as "Taxation," "Co-Determination in the Work-place," "Wage Earner Funds" (a volatile, hotly disputed issue in Sweden), "Who Owns Sweden?" and "Questions about the Future." All these issues are related to SAP ideological positions. In support of its Idéforums, SAP publishes attractive, well-illustrated, forty-page issue books with the background on each issue and the choices members face. SAP local study organizers organize their circles through ABF, encouraging both party members and the public to attend.

Idéforums is one of the only issue discussion programs in Sweden that uses some form of reporting mechanism. SAP generates feedback from study circle members on the issue under discussion by placing opinion questionnaires in the books and encouraging participants to send letters to SAP. Ahltorp said he receives five to six letters daily on the issues from local participants, usually party members, but he quickly went on to point out that the " 'Radslag' [issue ballots] and the reporting-back mechanisms are not the most important results of the SAP Idéforum circles; most important instead is what happens both in people's minds and in local follow-up. These types of circles often lead to action, and attitudes have been changed from the interchange and exposure to the materials."

Similarly, LO, usually in cooperation with a "Central Union Studies Committee," develops its own issues for circle discussion, mainly on political and trade union questions (e.g., "Your Rights at Work," "The National Economy"). It works closely with Brevskolan to publish and distribute materials, cooperates with ABF in forming study circles and receiving the government subsidy, and urges its trade union study organizers to form study circles at the work sites, usually on company time.

Brevskolan can also initiate some materials for issue discussion in the study circles; this is usually done under the auspices of ABF. Brevskolan developed an idea, for instance, for a discussion on "The National Economy." The interlocking issues committee then approved the materials; Brevskolan financed them; and ABF, LO, SAP, and KF publicized them to their local study circles. Ulf-Göran Widqvist, who observed that "the labor movement depends on study circles," said that the seventeen thousand copies of the issue book were ordered mainly because the study organizers recruited heavily and pushed it in local circles. He concluded (in a statement that directly reflected Gosta Vestlund's 1981 research study), "I envision increased public interest in issue discussion, and even in circles dealing with cultural programs, we find members going on to discuss issues and becoming more politically involved."

On the other hand, in its "Tjänsteman '80" national issues program in 1980, TBV, representing the white-collar and civil service employees, offers a graphic example of an issue discussion program that fell short of its sponsor's expectations. According to Leif Klint, the association, in cooperation with the Central Organization of Salaried Employees (TCO) with a membership of one million workers, every decade takes on a "big-scale, national project of public issue discussion for its study circles."

Designed by TBV and TCO for the members (Klint noted that "many of the civil servants are deeply interested in civic affairs"), the 1980 national program included eight issue books supplemented by local materials on such topics as taxation, working, education, transportation, and future studies. Klint candidly assessed the program:

TBV and TCO reach a reasonably educated population, 70 percent with a high school or postsecondary education, and the organizations conduct thirty thousand study circles annually. But the top officials were too fond of textbooks for the issues program. The members didn't like the texts, the study organizers didn't sell the program, and the members voted with their feet. These white-collar workers obviously didn't see a need for the program, or just were not interested in these issues.

Klint made some other observations. He said TBV expected fifteen thousand circle participants, but only five thousand showed up—"We couldn't excite the civil servants on these issues." Looking for reasons, he said, "We failed to consult them in advance, getting away from our own principles, so they simply ignored the project. We tried to impose it from the top." The lack of response to TBV's major initiative was an embarrassment to the sponsoring officials, and Klint thought "mention of the project still triggers a strong reaction by TCO members. But we learned from it. We should have let it develop, starting small. We tried too much."

Several other national associations also focus some efforts on civic affairs and issue discussion programs for their circles, and according to the testimony of several association officials, they plan to increase their programs on public issue discussion. Their reasoning is clear. There are extra government grants for study circle work on civic affairs, and these officials strongly believe that Sweden's educated adult population can benefit from greater understanding of complex public issues, even though adults receive much of their information from television and radio. Almost everyone I talked to believed the study circle is still Sweden's most efficient and powerful civic education format for increased public understanding of complex issues.

Still, pressures on the national associations and their study organizers are great for more aesthetic and cultural pursuits. "Our machinery is there, the networks are functioning," said Anders Höglund,

> but people do not automatically go to circles on civic affairs. This is a "How to . . ." era; people are turning inward—boats, cars, vacation homes. They simply don't care as much about public life. If you offer a study circle on "science policy," they stay home. If it's "How to Stay Healthy," they come out. All of the national associations are aware of this need to involve the public more in issue discussion. We need a renewal in this area.

SV, alone among the national associations, has introduced the concept of "theme years," designed according to its literature "to improve people's awareness of the world around us, . . . and of the importance of social and community understanding."[3]

And KFUK/M successfully used a Swedish Educational Broadcasting Company (UR) television program on "Violence on TV" in its study circles. In commenting on this program, Lena Samuelsson stated:

> People have to acquire enough information to affect the decision-making process, and study circles on civic issues will surely grow, especially on local issues, as people take increasing responsibility for their lives. But you can't impose the issues on them. . . . It won't work.

KFUK/M, in its statement of purpose, clearly states under the title, "A political engagement with society":

We wish to contribute towards an engagement
by our members in political work. Society
changes with increasing speed. This development creates new situations with new problems.
We wish to engage in those questions which
people experience as urgent. This is best done by
participating in the democratic decision-making
process. In the movement we engage in questions
related to the formation of the local environment.[4]

Regarding the use of the media in civic affairs study
circles, UR's Eddie Levin admitted to "an uneasy relationship between the national associations and the
government-supported broadcasting industry," for, as
he put it, "each association has its distinct point of
view, and it is difficult to develop programs to suit
them all; yet this is the nature of our TV media." UR
has a joint advisory committee with the associations
and often asks them what they need and how television
and radio can assist, "but it is much more difficult to
produce programs on controversial issues than it is to
produce programs on languages or other cultural issues," said Levin. By way of illustration, Gunilla
Sterner-Kumm of UR mentioned a radio series developed by UR called "How to Get People Speaking
Out on Issues." The tapes were used extensively by
ABF study organizers, but a problem arose with the
study circle leaders, "who didn't know how to effectively integrate radio programs into their circles."

Sterner-Kumm said television channels 1 and 2 (both
government sponsored) have periodic public issue discussions, but "there is no link to the study circles. The
interest is out there, the public calls in, but we haven't
linked up with the circles, and this is one of our challenges." She recalled one television special, "Swedes
and Immigrants," which was a controversial look at

the relationship between the Swedish public and immigrants, particularly Syrians:

> It was a sensitive subject, and we knew people watched, but it was too controversial for many of the study organizers. The public will discuss literature on TV but feels uneasy with controversial issues. The exceptions might be the trade unions and some of the left political parties.

Patrick Breslin believes television and radio could enhance ABF's study circle work, calling the media the "missing links" in study circles, even though UR is ready and interested in working with the study circles. Breslin places the blame on the associations and study organizers "who are holding back from fully exploiting the media potential."

According to Sterner-Kumm, the public gets its information elsewhere on public issues, not from study circles, and "Sweden needs more time to develop pedagogical methods of interrelating the media with study circles to encourage 'critical listening' and 'two-way interaction.' " Her hope lies in the development of "public-access neighborhood radio channels." Experiments in this media are taking place in fifteen neighborhoods throughout Sweden, with broadcasting rights extended to voluntary organizations—charitable groups, religious groups, community action groups, labor unions, and political parties—for local content: "The main aim of neighborhood radio is to afford local organizations an inexpensive and effective means of reaching their members and sympathizers within the broadcast radius, approximately five kilometers."[5]

The government recently moved to investigate the possibility of introducing public-access neighborhood television, along with cable TV, and these experiments could affect the way study circles address public issues in the future. The media can provide substantial information, but the key question will be how to maintain the integrity of self-directed learning through face-to-face discussion while integrating television—essentially effective as a one-way form of communication—into study circle deliberations.

Study organizers are not bound by the programs of their parent national associations. In the quest for study circle participants, organizers will assist anyone to form a circle on any local topic, as long as it does not exceed the admittedly broad boundaries of the national association's profile and mission. Thus we find Swedes turning to study circles as a primary instrument for bringing citizens together for discussion whenever there is a community need for airing, understanding, and often organizing around a pressing public issue. For example, Norman Eiger of Rutgers University notes that after the 1977 Co-Determination Act went into effect, worker-directors were asked to enroll in study circles in their local unions or district—on company time—to study such topics as Swedish corporate law, producer and consumer cooperatives, power relationships, and how a company functions.[6]

Leif Klint of TBV mentioned a small town in southern Sweden where a local union official became concerned when a plant threatened to close down, which would have removed the town's main livelihood. The official proceeded to organize ten study circles of employees, managers, and town officials, along with interested citizens from the town—all subsidized by ABF's circle grants—to discuss alternatives. They examined all aspects of the situation, called in experts, and pooled their results in another circle made up of representatives of the ten original circles. They then confronted the plant directors with their findings and communitywide support and thus succeeded in reversing the decision, opting for a plan of employee-shared ownership. In this instance, one concerned worker, using the study circle format and resources, was able to mobilize ideas and people, and helped an entire town keep its economic base.

KFUK/M's Lena Samuelsson provided another recent example of the use of the study circle to confront a neighborhood issue. The local municipal government in Örebro, a town in the heart of Sweden, wanted to rebuild the town center, but when a few residents saw the plans, there was no park, no green space on the drawings. So a group of citizens met in a rented apartment in a study circle sponsored by KFUK/M to discuss including "green areas" in plans for the center. After meeting several weeks, as study circles do, they presented alternatives to the city and won: "They acquired the knowledge," said Samuelsson, "to affect the decision and change it." She went on: "This type of study circle will grow as people see a need to increasingly share responsibility for their lives with the bureaucracy. They need alternatives, and in this instance, they found their alternatives through discussion and collective action."

Eiger refers to this form of issue discussion as "crisis education," citing a number of examples from Sweden when a local crisis—a strike, a threatened plant closing, layoffs—presented an opportunity for community learning.[7] Plant closings, both here and abroad, are traumatic for individuals and communities, generating feelings of powerlessness, depression, and communitywide alarm. When this happens in Sweden, workers, friends, and neighbors tend to seek collective study, alternatives, and then action by getting together in study circles, the easiest format for quick assembly on an issue. These crisis education circles are usually sponsored by one of the national associations and often involve the media. One example Eiger provides illustrates the power of collective ideas. The steelworkers at Viksmannshuttan, a medium-sized town three hours' drive from Stockholm, were faced with an imminent closing of their plant. They organized study circles and immediately brought in two television documentary producers from UR to work with the study circles to investigate how the proposed shutdown would affect the town. The study circles were able to document the foundry workers' craft on videotape, put together an exhibition for the community, and examine alternative uses for the plant. The documentary on the workers' skills in making steel products was shown throughout Sweden, and as a result of the circles' discussion, the plant was redesigned to assemble finished products. The workers learned something about the use of television, but they also learned that research, study, and discussion can lead to practical action, and that they can influence public life.[8]

Other examples of study circles addressing local issues were sprinkled throughout the interviews. It seems that whenever Swedish citizens, workers, or neighbors are faced with a major issue in their communities or in the workplace, the answer is found in collective thought and action arising out of study circle participation.

Use of films and drama in the study circles is becoming more popular. Inger Olsson of Skådebanan, an organization supported by the government to promote cultural activities among workers, talked about how some circles are even using theater to dramatize public issues such as international peace. She cited another example where workers witnessed Brecht's *Galileo* and used the performance as part of their discussion on the responsibility of scientists.

The Swedes know that in the study circles they have both an effective tool for local democracy and a way to bring citizens together to discuss local, national, and international issues. Still, the national leaders I talked to seemed hesitant about advocating use of the study circle network to address controversial issues, preferring to leave these discussions to spontaneous local initiative. There was also the lingering fear of government agencies using the study circles for information campaigns or creating "advocacy circles." Cultural programs—music, ceramics, languages—are safer and less open to controversy and public criticism. Yet throughout my interviews, I detected an undercurrent of interest in how to enhance study circle use in civic affairs programs as well as in how to capitalize on the media in collaboration with study circles in issue-oriented discussions.

Moreover, the Swedes have enthusiastically supported the export of their study circle model, especially to Third World countries, for use in issue discussion and literacy programs. To this end they have provided materials, funds, and specialists.

In one example, Tanzania, a socialist country under Julius Nyerere, who was recognized throughout the Third World for his strong advocacy of adult education for nation building and development, faced a population in the late 1960s that was 80 percent illiterate. With Swedes training the discussion leaders and providing basic materials and administrative help, Tanzania launched several small issue campaigns in 1969 (on the national development plan), 1970 (citizen voting), and

1971 (the tenth anniversary of the revolution). In 1973, Tanzania launched her first mass campaign—"Mtu ni Afya" (Man is Health)—and two million adults participated in it.

Budd Hall, of the International Council for Adult Education, reports that the 1973 campaign was designed to increase public awareness about health issues, to encourage group action on health matters, and to raise the nation's literacy rate.[9] Tanzania formed a national coordinating committee with representatives from the National Institute of Adult Education, the trade unions, political party leaders, and other agencies of government. They planned for eighteen months and trained seventy-five thousand study circle leaders.

The campaign, which lasted over twelve weeks, consisted of weekly radio programs, issue booklets on health, a leader's manual, and seventy-five thousand local study circles in towns and villages across the country. The circles met weekly, listened to radio programs, read the booklets, discussed both, and analyzed the ideas brought out by the materials and the leader.

Subsequent campaigns using the same structure were launched in 1975 on food habits and growing patterns, and in 1980 on afforestation. By 1981, Tanzania could claim a literacy rate of 80 percent, much of it attributable to the issue campaigns and the study circle movement.

It is noteworthy that, just as Sweden used the study circles some ninety years ago to increase literacy, overcome undereducation, and develop political awareness in its population, Tanzania, along with other developing countries such as Swaziland, Nicaragua, and Portugal, has turned to the same format for the same purposes—and has found it still to be an efficient tool for adult civic education. As Julius Nyerere said in

1974, in a statement that could easily apply to all developing countries and that seems to capture the essence of the study circle movement,

> The purpose of education is liberation through the development of man as a member of society . . . , thus making him aware of his potential as a human being, living in harmony with his neighbors and his environment.[10]

5

. . . .

Reflections
On Swedish Study Circles

Swedish research in adult education is oriented toward assessing and ultimately changing practice. But
there have been few methodologically oriented studies
of the Swedish study circles. Most reports from both
Swedes and visitors, mostly Americans, have uncriti-
cally praised the study circle movement and encouraged its duplication abroad—whether in developing
countries like Tanzania, or in a highly developed,
technologically advanced nation like the United States.
Several respondents in this study, however, referred
me to Jan Byström's study, *All Study Circles Are Not
Study Circles*, and to other attempts to gain some insights into this complex phenomenon beyond the anec-
dotal evidence that tends to pose for research. Such
self-criticism is especially valuable because any assessment of Swedish study circles and of their feasibility
in the United States must take into account the research that has been done by the Swedes themselves
on their study circles as well as the principles that
have driven the study circles and account for their

longevity as a treasured educational institution in Sweden's social democratic society.

Jan Byström, for example, funded by the National Swedish Board of Education, concerned himself with study circles for the undereducated, which were mainly sponsored by ABF and Brevskolan. What Byström found in his review of the study circle literature, his interviews with study circle officials and leaders, and his observations of study circles in action led him to conclude that many circles deviate from the ideal espoused in the literature of the national associations—cooperative study, personal growth, self-direction, and the leader as guide, not teacher.[1]

Byström met up with circles he describes as the "school class," the most common form of deviation with passive members and an instructing teacher. Byström blames this kind of group partly on unprepared leaders and partly on overregulation and direction from the national associations, which thereby limit circle members' input into planning. This situation is even more pronounced when the leader is also a "content expert," which contributes to greater member insecurity and dependency. Byström also refers to the "coffee party," in which the social milieu and camaraderie are more important than what is learned, and to the "therapeutic group," in which individual mental or social problems dominate the circle content.

Byström cites several other studies that show that "lack of time" is the primary reason for circle dropouts, although fear of new experiences ranks close behind as an inhibiting factor. Moreover, apprehension tends to make circle participants, especially newcomers, dependent on the leader as "teacher" rather than "guide" and undercuts full member participation. He mentions other studies as well that show how different study circle leaders approach the same subject in different ways, and he cites an elaborate study of seven trade union circles that holds up an ideal process of member interaction:

> Both leaders and members possessed experience on which the work of the circle can be based. . . . Above all, there was a clear linkage with the members' work places. The prospect of making practical use of the knowledge acquired and of transforming their conditions were powerful motive forces behind the members' studies. In these circles, differences of experience and background between members were regarded as an asset.[2]

But according to Leif Klint of TBV, "Contrary to popular opinion, study circles are not automatically democratic organizations. Democracy might emerge, but often the local circle needs time to jell, and its progress depends to a large part on the leader's style and preparation."

Byström maintains that three critical factors influence the success of a study circle: the importance of the circle leaders and of preparing them for their roles; common objectives between the leader and members; and the link between the knowledge and skills required and their application in the member's life. Both Klint and Byström, along with other respondents in this study, agreed on the complexity of the leader's role in the study circle, the need for the leader to meet periodically with other leaders, and the need for increased recognition and support from the associations to remove feelings of isolation and neglect.

Some of Byström's recommendations include better leader training in study circle methodology, better

leader instruction in the use of materials provided by
the national associations, encouragement of a positive
group atmosphere in which everyone's opinion counts,
sensitivity as to when intervention or restraint is called
for, and variety in the circle's activities. It goes without
saying that leaders should also be familiar with the
subject matter.

The Committee on Methods Testing in Adult Education, a government-appointed research committee, established 110 study circles in 1974 for 1,045 participants
in different parts of the country and reported on the
characteristics participants most desired in leaders.[3]
The most important quality "was to be able to clearly
pass on knowledge to the participants," which apparently confirmed Byström's findings that in many circles
members treat the leaders as content specialists and
teachers, rather than as discussion leaders and guides.
Participants also wanted their leaders to behave "so
they didn't have to worry about making fools of themselves," wanted circles at the workplace at least in
part on company time, and wanted circles close to their
neighborhoods.

In addition, participants in the experiment overwhelmingly felt their circles lived up to their expectations. A large proportion believed direct contact by
the study organizer motivated them to join the circles,
and they felt organizers should be drawn from the
trade unions and other popular movements in touch
with people's lives. They also recommended that the
associations work directly with local groups—the
handicapped, tenants, political party members—in
soliciting members to join the circles.

SFHL's Allan Sundqvist offers some structural criti-
cisms of the national associations, asking whether they
have been doing all they could to meet the growing

need for training of new circle leaders, for new materials for the circles, and for good research on the results of the circles' activities. Additionally, Sundqvist poses some hard questions. While admiring the extensive administrative structures of the national associations, with growing numbers of full-time officials at all levels, he asks if their increasing bureaucratization, abetted in part by increased governmental regulations and accountability needs, conflicts with the nature of the associations as "popular movements." He also cites critics who "have asked whether it is necessary and practical to have so many educational associations . . . working side by side in the same city or town," and he questions the initiative of some national associations for "producing their own study materials or otherwise distinguishing their activities from those of the other associations."

Finally, Sundqvist questions how broad the content is in local study circles, whether there is adequate association and study circle response to new public issues as they arise, and whether the circles are broadening their participant bases or resting on their laurels and tested constituencies.[4]

In a paper presented to a national seminar during the "Scandinavia Today" series in 1982, which was supported by the National Endowment for the Humanities, Bengt Göransson, Swedish minister of education and cultural affairs since 1982, talks about culture and education in contemporary Sweden, the popular movements, regionalization and decentralization, and the tensions between those "who favor a purely grass-roots popular movement model, and those . . . who want a cultural policy defined and administered by either local governments or the state."[5]

The same dilemma confronts those who plan and

carry out study circle activities. Given the Swedish public's acceptance of strong central government and bureaucracy (Leif Klint commented, "We Swedes have become accustomed to strong central government and bureaucracy in our lives") in contrast with its deep concern for freedom as exemplified in the oft-noted "free and voluntary" nature of the study circles, more than one respondent criticized the overbureaucratization and the lack of spontaneity and innovativeness in Swedish life while praising the government's accomplishments. They faulted the overt identification with ideological positions taken by some of the national associations at the same time that they decried the tarnishing and decline of ideology and social commitment in public life. And they lamented the lack of public concern for public issue discussion and civic affairs despite having witnessed a massive outpouring of participants for the study circles in 1979 on the nuclear power question.

To many of those thus concerned about increasing government bureaucratization in and declining public commitment to study circles, fault can also be found in the lack of a strong link to the media and "distance education." The Swedes still seem to be searching for ways to reconcile the "free and voluntary" nature of the local circles—in which members determine content and use of materials—with the use of television, radio, and, to some degree, distance education. This latter format can include the media as well as long-distance phone lines.

It is true that UR produces programs on public issues, sometimes on its own, sometimes in cooperation with one of the national associations and its circles. Yet, UR has no assurance that the programs will be used in the study circles. As Rune Flinck, professor

at the University of Lund and a specialist in distance
education, observed about the use of the media:

> The question of who will receive the government
> subsidy and the competition for study circle par-
> ticipants seem to work against innovation and
> new ideas—especially when the ideas come from
> the outside. The national study associations and
> the study organizers tend to be conservative and
> traditional in this area.

Further exploration is obviously needed in Sweden
on how to accomplish the media-study circle linkup.
Traditionally, radio has been effectively used in combination with the study circles, but television, including
the recent experimental introduction of cable TV into
Sweden, poses a different set of challenges because of
its strong centralizing character and the bias it creates
for passive viewing and one-way communication—both
anathema to study circle principles and methodology.

In our conversations, Swedish officials discussed
such formats as study circle "listening posts" tied in
with national or local television and radio (made easier
by UR experiments with "neighborhood radio channels" and the possibilities cable TV opens up for local
television production), increased use of TV/radio
documentaries for the circles, television critiques of
circles in action, and the sharing of ideas through new
video technologies. Television has become the central
focusing medium of our times in the United States and
abroad, and it will be used more and more as supplemental to the study circles, but it will only be effective
and in the spirit of study circle discussion if it is used
on the study circles' terms.

In other forms of distance education, some pioneer-
ing work is being done by Rune and Agneta Flinck of

the University of Lund. For example, the Flincks informed me that the Swedes are experimenting with
two-way telephone "teleconferencing," yet even this
type of low-key experimental work draws problems.
Rune Flinck talked about one such effort and the dif-
ficulties in finding association sponsorship:

> We received some funding from the Bank of
> Sweden to experiment with study circles using a
> two-way telephone hookup. I went to several of
> the national study associations to see if there was
> interest in sponsoring the circles, and none would
> pick up on it. I was informed time and again that
> "it would not work."

Almost no one mentioned the use of the newspaper
as a stimulus for study circle discussion, yet in a recent
report Stockfeldt and Sköld try to address the use of
this untapped resource. They refer, for example, to
"inserting a special study feature . . . on the center
pages of a newspaper" to enable every member to get
access to the study material. The advantages are that
costs can be kept low, sequential material can appear,
other sections such as the editorial page can be supportive, a dialogue on the issue can occur between the
editorial staff and the study circle participants, and a
long-term relationship can be created to mutual advantage of both the print media and the study circles.[6]
Even so, from my interviews, there does not seem to
be widespread interest in the newspapers as a resource
for the circles, although some officials expressed interest in trying to exploit this medium.

Yet perhaps the biggest criticism facing study circles
today ironically grows out of its successes. The
Swedish study circle movement was founded on the
radical premises of the popular movements—adult edu-

cation for liberation, for lifting an individual's sights, for preparing participants for citizenship, and for providing the basis for a more socially just and equal society. In just under a century, it has succeeded beyond the furthest imaginations of the founders. Today the Swedes are comfortable. Almost everyone I interviewed was at ease with his or her status, income, and quality of life.

Nevertheless, in a social democratic society where 95 percent of the citizens vote as their "civic duty," the Swedes are now growing uneasy with their adult education system as they search for ways to rekindle the founding spirit of civic consciousness to overcome, as one respondent put it, "increasing materialism, rampant individualism, misspent leisure time, and lack of involvement in public life." Gosta Vestlund asked: "Are our study circles still teaching involvement and empowerment, or assimilation and accommodation with the Swedish system? If we don't care about change, we are in effect giving over power to people who are worse politicians."

The national association officials interviewed were pleading for increased attention in their circles to civic affairs, but they admitted that competition for study circle members and dreams of a middle-class, increasingly affluent adult population often led the study organizers to reject their pleas in favor of increased cultural, aesthetic, and "value-free" adult education. Vestlund laid some of the blame squarely in the laps of the associations: "The associations' functionaries have often imposed 'top-down' issue programs on their circles, and the local circle leaders have refused to comply on principle."

Jan Ahltorp of SAP put it another way: "With our increasing affluence and leisure time, there is a real cleavage between the well educated and the not-so-well educated, and local circles are reflecting this split." Ahltorp's concern, echoed by other respondents and not unlike concerns expressed by adult educators in the United States and other industrialized nations, may reflect a larger dilemma for Sweden's national associations and study circle movement.

As an advanced social democratic society like Sweden becomes more affluent and comfortable (the "I made it, so leave me alone" mentality) and therefore more resistant to and suspicious of change, how do the study circles maintain the original premises based on equality and social justice that spurred the popular movements to launch them in the first place? Or can the study circles accommodate the new demands emerging from Sweden's modern social, educational, and cultural context?

Paulo Friere of Brazil wrote *Pedagogy of the Oppressed* to urge the conscious use of adult education to liberate undereducated, powerless people. Adult education should be "liberating education," in Friere's words; it should serve to empower and enhance individual capabilities through self-growth.[7]

In a later work, Friere saw the ideal adult education setting as a group of people who, through dialogue, come to understand the concrete situation in which they exist, the reasons for this situation, and possible solutions. The participants must create the curriculum along with the teacher, and the dialogue, which should be between political equals (regardless of age, class, or book learning versus practical, worldly experience), should provide "problem-posing" education for political and social governance.[8] Friere could have been describing the Swedish study circle movement.

The Swedes quote Friere frequently and relate his

writing to early twentieth-century Sweden and the beginnings of the study circle in the popular movements. Popular mass education, ideologically oriented, to liberate people and bring them into full participation in social, economic, and political life—these were the founding ideals on which Sweden's adult education movement and social democratic experiment were based. They remain the basic principles for contemporary adult education in Sweden.

Yet, as previously noted, the success of Sweden's modern educational system together with the country's high educational levels, relative affluence, and solid middle-class strengths have led to increasing public demands for more cultural and leisure-time adult education pursuits. And many of those interviewed for this study, while acknowledging the original goals of the study circle founders and their populist ideals, have been grappling with the dichotomy that modern practice has created.

In reality, two-thirds of Sweden's annual 325,000 study circles have a social or cultural focus, and many of the officials interviewed fear that the public, as well as some officials in the national associations, have moved away from the study circle movement's popular roots. These concerns were most pronounced in my interviews with the trade union, SAP, and government officials, but almost all respondents thought the Swedish government and the national associations should be doing more to encourage increased attention in the study circles to civic affairs and consideration of pressing public issues.

Even so, we should consider how far the Swedish study circle movement has come over its ninety-year existence: its stability, its pervasiveness, and the public's acceptance of it as a way of life. Over 150,000

Swedish citizens turned out on short notice for the nuclear power discussions in 1979. Numerous local circles, perhaps up to 10 percent of the total circles annually, focus on local issues, and the media actively promotes public issue discussion programs. The evidence is clear: the Swedish study circle phenomenon is alive, healthy, and the envy of practicing adult and civic educators in many other countries. Every adult Swede has an opportunity, in fact multiple opportunities, to participate in well-organized, adult civic education programs each year through study circles of their own choosing. In this sense, Sweden is a "learning society" with a strong emphasis on civic literacy and competence, even though some study circle officials are urging even more emphasis on civic affairs.

Yet we should also recognize that, outside of the Scandinavian folk high schools, university general extension and Agricultural Cooperative Extension programs, YMCA-YWCA adult programs, and a few others like the United States' "Great Decisions" program, most adult education movements experience cycles of boom and bust based on their times and the national mood. This was as true for the Holbrook Lyceum Movement of the early 1800s as it was for the "tent Chautauquas" of the first quarter of the twentieth century, the Studebaker forums of the mid-1930s, or the group dynamics people in the 1950s and early 1960s (see chap. 6). Sweden, however, remains "a study circle democracy," in Olof Palme's words. Thus, since the study circle remains Sweden's primary mechanism for adult civic education and for adult education in general, the question has to be asked: What accounts for its longevity, its ninety-year-old vitality?

A popular organizational base in society. The popular

movements of the early 1900s—labor unions, temperance groups, and free church groups, along with the YMCA-YWCAs and the Social Democratic party—gave birth to the Swedish study circle in a time of great social unrest and early industrialization. The ten national associations that now sponsor study circles, all with strong government support, are rooted in a broad popular and institutional base in Swedish society. And because they are grounded in the society, these associations provide organizational legitimacy for the study circles, appeal to their own constituencies for participation so they have built-in audiences, and are eager to impress the public with their study circle offerings so as to expand their circle activities.

The strength and importance of the popular movements in Sweden can be illustrated, in Peter Engberg's opinion, by contrasting the Swedish situation with neighboring Finland. Because they articulated the public's fears, hopes, and desire for change and because they developed the leadership to run the country—mostly through their study circles—the Swedish popular movements, according to Engberg, "saved our country from internal strife, civic war, and possible revolution." As he explained:

> In 1918, the Finns had a civil war between the leftist Red Guard and the conservative White Guard, and deep scars remained. Even after independence in 1920, political instability remained until the 1930s, with periodic extreme swings of power.
>
> Labor was always an outsider in Finland, and they don't talk about popular movements the way we do; they are not part of the democratic structure of the country as they are here. Less

than one in ten Finns gets involved in adult education annually, their adult education associations
are weak, and the popular movements do not
apply any pressure for change. Here, they pre-
cipitated social and political change.

A participant-centered small group format. The study
circle format is simple, straightforward, democratic, and
voluntary. It puts the burden for adult education where
it belongs—on the individual adult participant. It has
flexibility and mobility; it encourages participation and
self-directed learning; and it is usually nonthreatening,
an important aspect for adults uncomfortable with formal school settings.

There is no elaborate set of procedures or complicated methodology connected with the circles. The
pedagogy consists of a set of behavioral principles, and
no elaborate, sophisticated advanced training or de-
grees are necessary for the circle leaders or participants. It is a people's format in which all participants
can perceive themselves as equals. And it has the advantage of an integrating national network concerned
only with study circle adult education and advancement
achieved through circles that reflect the organizational
mission and programs of the national associations.

National government support. Another factor contributing to the durability of the study circle movement
is the substantial government support available to the
ten national associations through annual grants based
on their study circle activity. This permits the associations to have an administrative structure conducive
to running a national program. The public knows it is
paying for this apparatus and for subsidizing the local
circles, but since so many citizens participate, the pub-

lic remains supportive no matter who is running the government. The Liberal government that took power in 1976, for example, left the subsidies untouched, partly because their affiliated association, SV, was also a beneficiary.

The associations have great flexibility in their circle programs, a factor which also contributes to the movement's vitality. Most, because of their profiles, emphasize certain themes or give special focus to their circle activity, and there seems to be enough variety for everyone. According to Kurland, "What this approach presupposes . . . is that the themes are sufficiently compelling to attract participants to the circles and that the materials are sufficiently appealing to hold them once they join."[9]

This isn't always the case, as we have seen in TBV's "Tjänsteman '80" campaign, but overall the associations have earned public loyalty for their study circle offerings. The pluralism of the study circle movement ultimately benefits the public; they know what they are getting when they join a circle. It is essentially value-oriented adult education, but it works because citizens are free to choose which circle they want to join. And when circles address public issues, national or local, citizens can choose among a full spectrum of positions.

Flexibility and adaptability in content. The original Swedish study circles were aimed at the working class, the poor, the undereducated, and rural dwellers— people who had been excluded from the formal educational process—and these remain, along with the handicapped, the aged, and the new immigrants, strong priorities for the social democratic society. But as the Swedish population has attained higher levels of edu-

cation, as the people have moved to the cities with
their intellectual and artistic attractions, and as the
public "has become increasingly individualistic and
self-interested with a 'leave me alone' attitude," in
Gosta Vestlund's words, study circles have adapted to
offer more cultural and aesthetic subjects. The circles
are part of society, and by meeting the new demands,
they have been able to survive.

But the Swedes have not forgotten what originally
motivated the study circle movement, be it their concern with the generations of adults who have not received the required nine years of formal schooling or
with the about-to-be unemployed who attend circles
to learn new job skills. Moreover, in his 1981 research
study, Gosta Vestlund demonstrated that up to a third
of the participants in any form of study circle go on to
become active in civic and political life beyond the circle. As Vestlund told me, "functioning in social groups
of any sort helps people to become self-reliant, in-
creases their communication skills, helps them to set
agendas and determine the course of their studies, and
encourages through their leadership roles enhanced
feelings of self-worth."

Vestlund mentioned that following his study, several
highly placed respondents, concerned with the drift
away from civic affairs and the lack of concern for issue
discussions, decided to overcome their opposition to
increased cultural programming in the circles and accept the fact that the associations depend on public
support for circle participants. Besides, they were a
little more comfortable in the knowledge that many of
those participants in the cultural circles would invariably go on to increased activity in civic life.

A continuing relationship with public issue discussion and national life. Despite the emphasis on cultural and aesthetic subjects, continuing use of the study circle format as a means of encouraging adult Swedes to become familiar with pressing issues of the times has enabled the circles to adapt and remain a force for informed public opinion and social change. The government, the national associations, and the Swedish public have accepted the study circle format as an effective means to stimulate informed public views on national, local, neighborhood, and workplace issues.

Respondents stressed time and again, however, the difficulty of attracting the public to civic affairs programs. The Swedish public has many alternative forms of access to information about issues, especially television, and they face the same competitive entertainment demands on their leisure time as we do—television, movies, sports, increased travel, vacations, second homes, and well-supplied bookstores. These respondents saw themselves in a constant struggle to keep civic affairs circles prominent in their work and to find effective ways to recruit a reluctant public. Without this thrust for civic affairs and the periodic national issue campaigns, I believe the study circles would lose some of their vitality as "small democracies" and would become, as much adult continuing education in the United States is today, a convenient means to use leisure time, to permit those with education to indulge their educational interests, and to forget that one of the continuing needs of any democratic society is awareness and vigilance on the part of the governed.

Swedish officials at all levels seemed to accept without question the critical role the study circle can play in assisting Swedish adults to become integrated into the decision-making process. Be it the national referendum on nuclear power, the public's views on computer power, a trade union's position on a plant closing, a municipality's land use policy, or a television documentary on the new immigrants—the Swedes invariably turn to the study circle as a proven format for education and action, for a reflection of the average citizen's judgment on the issue.

The structural contrast becomes evident: in one of the world's most highly centralized, bureaucratized societies, the study circle—a microcosm of fundamental democracy—has helped to keep the Swedish bureaucracies, both public and private, responsive, while providing individual citizens with that feeling of self-worth, self-reliance, and knowledge of their capacity to influence civic life. Such leadership and responsibility in citizens is essential to democratic participation and vital community life. Kurland sums it up in the following way: "As consensus emerges, leadership can then espouse a position in the political arena knowing it has behind it the collective wisdom ["public judgment" as we call it at the Kettering Foundation] of the average citizen."[10] In our civic education work with the National Issues Forums, we have used the term "political permission" to describe the policymaker's dependence on an informed public. Since most of the Swedish political leadership has come out of the study circle movement, they tend to take the study circles and their circle members seriously on public issues. This recognition provides an additional note of legitimacy for the study circle programs.

Sweden, one of the most egalitarian countries in the world, still encourages individual freedom, and she has found ways—primarily through her adult education movement and its two principal formats, the study circle and the folk high school—to encourage reform, change, and reasonably tolerable solutions to the problems faced by a modern, urbanized, industrialized and post-industrialized, knowledge-based and technologically oriented society. The Swedes have democratized culture and education in a way we all can envy.

Yet one finds undercurrents and restlessness as new challenges arise, such as the influence of technology and questions of international peace. One of the challenges Sweden faces is the export of its model of adult education, which is already finding its way to Third World countries as a revolutionary device for upgrading whole populations. As Rune Flinck advised, "Never take a system or an idea that works in one culture and hope to impose it intact in another."

In the next section, I will speculate on how the study circle concept, focusing on public issue discussion and civic affairs, could be adopted in the United States. The United States is not Sweden. We are not a homogeneous people, a unified society. We have a wealth of religions, languages, and cultures in our midst, often existing side by side. We inhabit a vast territory. We have multiple and competing forms of adult education, which the government believes should be self-supporting and without subsidy, with certain exceptions such as the national literacy program or job training. We have no sustained history or organized network of institutionalized programs that promote citizen education; much of our public issue discussion is informal and spontaneous, often in reaction to an immediate need (as in a public hearing on a highway cutting through a neighborhood or in a neighborhood task force on crime). In effect,

> the percentage of Americans taking part in even the most extensive forum efforts is miniscule

compared to Sweden. In a society where half the
people do not bother to vote and where only about
one-third read even one book a year, the numbers
willing to devote the time and energy to serious
study and discussion (of public policy issues) are
a small percentage of the population.[11]

By offering every adult Swede an opportunity to
participate in an adult learning experience of his or
her own choosing annually, and by creating opportunities through the study circles for exchanges of
ideas on issues that affect daily lives, the Swedes are
fulfilling a commitment to the value of knowledge and
an informed citizenry that every democratic society
should envy and perhaps copy. That is our lesson as
we turn to the history of small group discussion in the
United States and the implications for implanting the
study circle concept in our country.

STUDY CIRCLES, as they have grown in Sweden, Canada, and the United States, vary widely in format, size, setting, the make-up of participants, and the issues participants choose to address.

Leonard P. Oliver

Office workers in Stockholm meet for mutual benefit at lunchtime at Kungsträdgården (a public park).

Hans-Ola Larsson

More than 30 percent of all Swedish study circles are devoted to studying languages. These participants are studying Greek before embarking on a holiday in Greece.

Subsidized by the government, Sweden's ten national educational associations promote, organize, and conduct study circles on a wide range of subjects.

Lars-Håken Nilsson

Sponsored by TBV (Salaried Employees Educational Association), this group of trade union leaders is learning communication skills and argumentation.

Tore Persson

With its focus on environmental issues, this Sfr (Study Promotion Association) study circle gathers to discuss species preservation.

Another Sfr group takes a field trip to address
environmental issues firsthand.

ABF (Worker's Educational Association) gives
people with little formal schooling the opportunity to further their studies. These women
are training themselves in public speaking.

The International Union of Bricklayers and Allied Craftsmen conducted their first series of study circles in summer 1986. The focus was on problems facing the union and alternatives for the future as outlined in the BAC's Project 2000 Committee Report.

Issue booklets were developed by the BAC for each of their five study circle sessions.

Bricklayers and Allied Craftsmen

1986
Study
Circle
Program

SESSION 1
Where We Stand:
Challenges to Our Jobs
and Our Union

The
Craft is
Back

Leonard P. Oliver

Business agents of BAC local unions from the Northwest United States and Canada meet in Yakima, Wash.

Leonard P. Oliver

Local 4, one of the first Canadian BAC study circles, gathers in Montreal, Quebec.

The National Issues Forums, sponsored by the Domestic Policy Association, is the newest national program in the United States to further the goals of adult civic education. In their efforts to bring citizens into the policymaking process, the DPA/NIF community forums provide for a variety of reporting-back mechanisms.

Juliana Laufersweiler

"Welfare: Who Should Be Entitled to Public Help?" is the focus for this forum in Dayton, Ohio, one of two hundred local communities participating in the NIF's fall 1985 series.

DPA/NIF file photo

NIF brochures on the three issues of the 1986 series reflect the breadth of public policy topics that have stimulated small group forums.

Ray Gildea of the Stennis Institute of Government at Mississippi State University reports back to members of the U.S. Congress during "Washington Week" in April 1987.

Brian Lamb, C-SPAN (moderator); Robert F. McNamara, former secretary of defense; Lawrence J. Korb, former assistant secretary of defense, and Henry Kissinger, former secretary of state, participate in an NIF national teleconference on nuclear arms, held at the Lyndon B. Johnson Library, March 1984.

6

. . . .

Public Issue Discussion
In the United States

From the time our country was founded and our people given the monumental task of governing themselves—a hitherto untried experiment in popular government since the time of the Greek city-state—the American public has witnessed a continuing tension between our system of representative government and the demands for popular democracy. Our founders understood the fragility of democracy; they built in all kinds of checks and balances to prevent unbridled democratic power, yet they knew that success with democratic structures depended less on institutional checks than on the restraint and informed judgment of citizens educated in civic responsibility.

To further democracy through popular education on public issues of the day, religious, civic, and intellectual leaders have arisen periodically in our history to create structures and movements for public issue discussion and enlightenment. These structures, sponsored variously by private institutions, volunteer groups, and the government, have taken diverse forms reflective of their times.

Meeting together on shared interests and for common understanding and decision making goes back to our country's origins, when free men and women understood that public acceptance of decisions made by authorities was as important as efficiency of decision making. During the colonial-Revolutionary period, the practice of meeting together helped define the people's relationship to their government and to each other and gave the public a sense of common purpose leading up to the Declaration of Independence and the drafting and ratification of the Constitution.

Town meetings, for example, indigenous to American soil, provided one format for colonists to widely debate and resolve public issues. Open to all citizens, they were public institutions that Jefferson called "the wisest invention ever devised by the wit of man for the perfect exercise of government." They have been around since the early 1600s and, in one form or another, are still functioning legal bodies in many New England towns today, where local issues are debated by citizens attending the annual town meeting.

In 1727, Ben Franklin organized a series of weekly meetings—or juntos—in Philadelphia for influential citizens to discuss current affairs, civic life, topics such as citizenship and political liberty, and ways to remedy legal injustices. Juntos were started in other cities as well and eventually led to the formation of the American Philosophical Society.

Then in 1772, on the eve of the American Revolution, Sam Adams initiated the "Committees of Correspondence," which, along with the town meetings, served to maintain a constant flow of communications in the colonies and led directly to the Revolution; in essence, they drew authority to act from the people.

In the early 1800s, borrowing ideas from England

and her effort to spread learning and democracy to
working-class people, and fueled by the twin forces of
universal male suffrage and free popular education,
several movements arose in the United States to dis-
seminate knowledge to the adult population. The most
prominent of these was Josiah Holbrook's Lyceum
Movement. Beginning with his first lyceum in
Millburn, Massachusetts, in 1826, Holbrook wanted to
create a lyceum—an "adult learning center"—in every
town in the country for citizen discussion of public
issues and civic improvement. By 1835, he could point
to 3,500 local lyceums, all run democratically by local
citizens. The lyceums were strong advocates of free
public education, but faced with growing controversy
over slavery and increased competition from free-
wheeling lecturers, the movement died by midcentury.

However, the late nineteenth and early twentieth
centuries saw several adult education movements concerned with citizenship education arise simultaneously
as post–Civil War America witnessed expanded suffrage, waves of immigrants to be "Americanized," the
spread of knowledge through the land-grant universities, and the demands of the new urban society and
groups such as women fighting for equal access to educational opportunities. For example, Bishop John
Vincent launched his summer assembly at Lake Chautauqua, followed by the Chautauqua Literary and Scientific Circle (CLSC) in the 1870s, with the
"Chautauqua Movement" reaching its peak by 1915.
The previously cited fifteen thousand "home study circles" found in towns across America used education
and small group discussion to examine contemporary
issues as well as broader topics in the liberal arts.

Later, in the early decades of the twentieth century,
university general extension and Agricultural Coop-

erative Extension programs created models for bringing citizens together for discussions of public affairs
(mainly urban lecture series for general extension and
small group discussion in rural areas for Cooperative
Extension). Federal support of Cooperative Extension
provided federal funding for the first time for public
affairs programming.

In addition, the progressive movement of the late
nineteenth and early twentieth centuries saw urban
settlement houses, such as that founded by Jane
Addams, used as citizenship centers for the poor and
for the newly arrived immigrants. This was accompanied by the growth of women's clubs and groups like
the League of Women Voters, which sought to extend
popular education in civic affairs to previously disenfranchised adults. And just before World War I, Ford
Hall in Boston initiated public issue lecture-discussions,
which led to the creation of two hundred Open Forum
programs across the country. This movement
flourished briefly until the advent of the World War.

People in economic distress often turn to radical
economic and political measures, and the fear of
economic chaos at home and the influence of dictator-
ships abroad led to the development of a series of
government-sponsored public issue discussion programs during the Great Depression. The most extensive of these in our nation's history was the
"Studebaker Public Forum Movement," initiated in the
early years of the depression by John W. Studebaker,
commissioner of education under Roosevelt (1934–48).
Studebaker, formerly superintendent of schools in Des
Moines, Iowa, where he started his public forum movement, used federal funding to establish throughout
forty-two states a nationwide network of nineteen demonstration centers and 750 public forums for "adult

civic education." This network was sponsored by public school districts, public libraries, colleges and universities, and religious, political, and civic organizations. President Roosevelt recognized Studebaker's forums "as meeting places for the discussion of public questions in the cities, hamlets, and on the farms throughout the length and breadth of the land."[1] Following Studebaker's lead, the U.S. Department of Agriculture's Cooperative Extension Service launched a federally supported program of seventy "schools of philosophy" in thirty-nine states to train some forty thousand farm leaders annually. The training program led to extensive farmer discussion programs, which eventually reached two million farm people. It featured extensive literature on organizing and leading public issue discussion groups as well as issue-related pamphlets.

One other farmer-based discussion program that arose in these prewar years also gained national attention. In 1936, the Ohio Farm Bureau Federation (OFBF) created the Ohio Advisory Councils to bring small groups of farm families together in their homes for monthly discussions of important economic and political issues. The concept derived from several visits to Nova Scotia by OFBF officials, who observed firsthand St. Francis Xavier University Extension Department's program of study circles for impoverished fishermen to discuss common problems and seek solutions. The idea spread rapidly throughout Ohio, and the OFBF used the local advisory councils to help formulate farm policy. Discussions centered on monthly issue guides distributed by the OFBF. The OFBF's advisory councils are still a force for change in Ohio and in other states adopting the idea, with over seventeen hundred councils and thirty-four thousand indi-

viduals meeting monthly in small group discussion.
The advisory councils have been cited over the years
as models for strengthening democracy and for local
democratic participation in issues important to the
lives of farmers and their friends and neighbors.

When the patriotic national consensus surrounding
World War II softened regional, ideological, and
socioeconomic differences among the American public,
our single-minded purpose of winning the war seemed
to eliminate any pressing need to foster public issue
discussion. Some programs that were in existence,
such as the Studebaker forums, fell by the wayside,
whereas others, like the Ohio Advisory Councils, were
held in abeyance until the war ended. After World
War II ended, however, a series of major events—an
economic downturn, the beginnings of the Cold War,
nuclear proliferation, labor unrest, the Korean War,
the hysteria of the McCarthy era—triggered a new
range of public issue discussion programs.

Founded in 1947 through the University of Chicago,
the Great Books program is one of the oldest issue
discussion programs still functioning in the United
States, with more than twenty-five hundred discussion
groups and some five thousand annual participants.
These small groups, sponsored by churches, libraries,
colleges and universities, and corporations, encourage
participants both to apply ideas from the great books
to contemporary concerns and to develop the technique
of group study. Local institutions provide leader training and Leader's Guides, and offer each participant
boxed, paperbound sets of readings for the program
and leader's aids. The Great Books program, participant centered, democratic, and voluntary, can be
pointed to as a forerunner for the small discussion
group movement in the United States.

With support from the Ford Foundation's Fund for Adult Education, the American Library Association (ALA) in 1951 created the "American Heritage Project," an experimental program of adult discussion groups focused on public libraries. Its purpose was to enable libraries across the country to provide opportunities for adult discussion of contemporary social, political, and economic issues in the light of basic documents, ideas, and experiences from the American heritage. Discussions were based on readings and films, and local library discussion programs were encouraged and conducted by state library extension agencies, which also trained staff and discussion leaders, and provided materials. The ALA reported in 1955 that in the seventeen states receiving grants and the other sixteen participating informally, 1,474 discussion groups were formed reaching 28,500 participants. ALA trained 1,208 discussion leaders. Many of the participating libraries continued their discussion groups after the funding ceased.

The American Foundation for Continuing Education was created in 1951 as the American Foundation for Political Education and was subsequently renamed. Lasting for almost two decades, it developed materials for adults to use in study discussion programs on public issues of the day and on broad political, economic, and ideological themes. It also offered training and technical assistance to organizations, agencies, and local groups interested in developing study groups, and it placed special emphasis on discussion programs for business and industry. Aided by funding from the Fund for Adult Education, the foundation published many of its own discussion materials, including such works as *Readings in World Politics, Readings in American Democracy,* and *Economics and Politics,* along with case studies on current issues and discussion leaders manuals. Although the foundation created its own discussion group network, these materials found their way into adult civic education programs around the country. The foundation also worked closely with university extension programs, encouraging their participation. In one example, the University of California's University Extension Division conducted more than two hundred discussion groups in 1958 for over five thousand adult participants in such subjects as American Democracy, Great Issues in American Politics, and Economic Reasoning.

The Foreign Policy Association, founded in 1918, created its "Great Decisions" program in 1955 as an experiment to promote citizen awareness and small group discussion of foreign policy issues. The Great Decisions programs, still flourishing, are sponsored annually by regional FPA offices and cosponsored by public schools' adult education programs, libraries, independent Great Decisions committees, colleges and universities, Cooperative Extension, World Affairs Councils, metropolitan adult education councils, churches, and civic associations. Great Decisions, which in 1985 reported 150,000 adult participants in eight hundred communities, addresses eight issues every February and March. Newspapers, television, and radio stations develop programs surrounding the issues. Receiving sixty thousand opinion ballots annually from the discussions, Great Decisions then shares the results with congressional committees, State Department and other administration officials, and opinion leaders.

In the late 1950s, the Metroplex Assembly of St. Louis, sponsored by Washington University's Civic Education Center, developed a series of twice-yearly

television broadcasts on critical public issues. Key to
the program were organized viewing groups ("listening
posts") with trained discussion leaders, who watched
the television program (documentary, panel) for one-
half hour in branch libraries, community centers, college halls, churches, and private homes. The study
groups then discussed the issue for an hour and tele-
phoned the studio with questions that arose from their
discussions. These questions and resulting responses
from the television studio formed the second half of
the program. Viewing group leaders provided
background materials and discussion guides on the issues. Opinion ballots provided an additional feedback
mechanism for policymakers.

After the ferment of the late 1960s, with the national
debates, "teach-ins," workshops, mass rallies, and
other forums for discussion of social inequality, civil
rights, and the Vietnam War, the 1970s were reasonably tranquil. The Watergate affair rekindled our interest in public ethics, constitutionality, and the pow-
ers of the press, the presidency, and Congress. The
nation's bicentennial in 1976 provided a convenient context for what Walter Cronkite termed the "intellectual
side of the celebration," with the National Endowment
for the Humanities, following its success in creating
voluntary state councils across the country for public
issue discussion, taking up the challenge. NEH seemed
an ideal, neutral federal sponsor for a national debate
to follow Cronkite's dictum "that we understand who
we are before we look at who we should be."

During 1975–76, NEH initiated over one thousand
public issue discussion forums in cities and towns
across America in an attempt to involve a broad segment of the American public in a year-long discussion
of topics related to who we are and what policy issues

lie in our future. This program, the American Issues
Forum, created increased awareness of public forums
for issue debate and served as a catalyst for a wide
range of local forum experiments: television forums
with community "viewing groups"; library sponsorship
of neighborhood forums; weekly discussion groups in
churches, board rooms, labor union halls, and colleges
and universities; newspaper articles on the issues; and
community forums in prisons, senior centers, and even
in American embassies around the world. The American Issues Forum was one of the only bicentennial
programs to give intellectual purpose to the celebration, and many of the local forum programs continued
after the bicentennial period, often with the assistance
of state humanities councils.

    Following the American Issues Forum, NEH sup-
ported the American Association of Community and
Junior Colleges (AACJC) in several national discussion
programs centered in the community colleges. AACJC
used regional demonstration centers, concentrated on
linking the forums with the NEH's "Courses by Newspaper," and built a cadre of community colleges interested in public issue discussion. In 1978, NEH
funded AACJC to capitalize on the administration's
overriding concern with the energy issue in the late
1970s. AACJC expressed interest in using the community college as the focus for community forums, and
with NEH, Department of Energy, and corporate support, it mounted an intensive ten-week nationwide
public discussion on "Energy and the Way We Live."
After the program, which took place from February
to April 1980, AACJC reported 1,205 community
forums in forty-eight states sponsored by ten regional
"coordinating colleges" and four hundred local community colleges. Over one hundred thousand adults

participated, with another 9.4 million viewers and readers reached through the television and newspaper programs. AACJC received twenty-nine thousand completed questionnaires from the local forums balloting on our energy choices and shared the results with administration energy officials.

In the 1960s and 1970s, the antiwar, civil rights, consumer, and women's movements all reflected the public's increasing concern for more of a voice in public affairs. Citizen organizations can translate these feelings into debate and policy alternatives, and metropolitan Citizens Leagues have become effective vehicles for citizen research, education, discussion, and recommendations on issues affect our cities and states. Building on the experience of the Minneapolis–St. Paul Citizens League originated in 1952, volunteer Citizens Leagues have sprung up in some twenty-five metropolitan areas, most developing in the 1970s and early 1980s. These citizen-membership organizations, supported by member dues and corporate/foundation contributions, stress citizen research and debate on the issues, using citizen task forces and public forums to come up with policy recommendations. Citizens Leagues help to set the "community agenda," provide in-depth analysis and alternatives, and build community support and consensus for the recommendations. Citizens Leagues are expanding, and they hold promise of providing broad public understanding and participation in public issue discussion as well as ways to directly influence the policy-making process.

Our history of public issue discussion dramatically illustrates that, one way or another, the United States has continually sought to involve the average citizen in civic life. We are people accustomed to meeting and talking together about public life and issues, as evidenced by the plethora of forums and small discussion groups identified with movements for citizen understanding and popular democracy, and as such, we know that the more citizens can have access to essential information and debate about public issues, the more likely the government will make wise decisions. We have had a covenant with our government since our founding about tolerance of dissent, acceptance of individual and group opinions ("public judgment"), and public accountability, and we are likely to welcome the introduction of organized, sustained, and serious discussions—such as study circles—that perpetuate this covenant.

However, from the time of the New England town meetings in the colonial period to World War II, organizers of adult civic education programs—whether the Lyceum Movement, university extension, the "tent Chautauquas," or the Studebaker forums—seemed more comfortable with large public lecture halls and school auditoriums, and with public lectures and expert speakers or panels as their bread-and-butter format, than with small group discussion reaching limited numbers of participants. One explanation could be that our public forum movements tended to be imposed from institutions (e.g., university extension, American Library Association) or from the government (e.g., Office of Education, NEH) rather than develop spontaneously and group-by-group out of popular movements—out of the public's need for adult civic education—as they did in Sweden. Except for the early town meetings, local initiative was not the prime motivating force in our public forum movements, and it is questionable if any of the public forum programs cited earlier ever truly belonged to or were dependent on the support and good will of the American public.

Among the few exceptions to this historical pattern was the Chautauqua Literary and Scientific Circle (CLSC), described in chapter 1 and earlier in this chapter, which did develop a program of four-year correspondence study accompanied by "home study circles"—organized, rigorous reading and discussion in the liberal arts leading to college accreditation. By 1915, CLSC's fifteen thousand study circles helped shed light on public issues, in accordance with the philosophy that "issues and contemporary problems were to be treated philosophically, though in popular form."[2]

The CLSC study circles were based on the needs of an increasingly industrialized, urban population for knowledge, credentials, and the education that had passed them by in the formal school settings—a rationale similar to that which inspired the founding of the Swedish popular movements. Perhaps this is why the CLSC study circles were so attractive to Oscar Olsson of the Swedish temperance movement when he visited in 1898 that he was prompted to take the idea back to Sweden.

During World War II, sociologist Kurt Lewin and his followers pioneered small group discussions with housewives as a way to help the war effort by promoting rationing and the eating of organ meat. The method took hold with adult education groups and for several decades became the dominant form of adult education in the United States, called variously group dynamics, T-groups, workshops, work groups, encounter groups, sensitivity training, group therapy, task forces, buzz groups, and, more recently, "focus groups," which attempt to crystallize a single issue.[3] Thus, an entire generation of adult educators grew up in the 1950s and 1960s believing that adult education really entailed small group processes. The literature of the period is replete with such titles as "Group Processes for Adult Education," "The Workshop Way of Learning," "Learning to Work in Groups," and "Adult Education Groups and A-V Techniques."

Interest in small group work here did not arise from the public or popular movements as it did in Sweden, nor were most of those who adopted the small group discussion method in adult education motivated by a coherent social philosophy about participation in civic life or social change. Rather, interest in small group work was prompted by adult educators and their organizations interested in identifying with a distinct methodology divorced from the overriding concerns and issues of the day. Although many adult educators of the period believed small group discussion was the democratic way, the idea was never institutionalized into a national program, as it was in the Swedish study circles.

Swedish literature on study circles shows that the study circle innovators such as Oscar Olsson and Richard Sandler also led the popular movements concerned with undereducation, social unrest, and economic and political inequalities. Olsson, Sandler, and other popular movement leaders saw in the study circles a means, an instrument, with which to uplift the educational level of their adult members who had fallen outside the formal structures of education. They wanted to use study circles for self-education and to create a new society based on social justice and social equality. And they knew that an informed, active, and educated citizenry would be the vehicle for social and political transformation.

In this sense, study circles could not be divorced from larger principles of individual and community growth. From the start, they were perceived as "miniature democracies," fundamental to a democratic society and useful primarily in that they provided the people with the needed information and insights to enable them to participate and have an effective voice in decision making.

On the other hand, the only historical, long-running popular movements in the United States that have strong adult civic education programs and that, to some degree, parallel the Swedish popular movements are the churches with their adult discussion groups, the YMCA and YWCAs with their evening courses, the FPA's Great Decisions program on world affairs, the labor movement with its extensive programs of worker education, and Cooperative Extension with its vast cadre of county agents, home extension specialists, and rural–small town constituencies. Yet none of these movements consciously identifies with the field of adult education or recognizes small group discussion or study circles as a vital facet of its adult civic education work. And without this identification—without a rationale based on democratic principles and sociopolitical change for introducing study circles into their programs—they may be simply perceived as just another competing adult education methodology.

Norman Kurland of the New York State Education Department, on returning from Sweden in 1978 where he studied the study circles and worker education, initiated an extensive program of foundation-funded study circles through the New York State Study Circle Consortium. In a 1982 article about his work, "The Scandinavian Study Circle: An Idea for the U.S.," Kurland observes that even though the term *study circle* is new to our shores, certain groups such as the League of Women Voters, the YMCA-YWCA, the FPA's Great Decisions program, "Great Books" discussion groups, and others paved the way by using study circle-type formats.[4]

But it is not a conscious concept, as it is in Sweden. Again, we have no coherent history or philosophy about study circles in our country, and the term has not been used to convey the idea of systematic, sustained study and the relationship of adult education through study circles to practical affairs and sociopolitical change.

Kurland thought study circles could "help solve some of our current problems" and serve as "a systematic means for engaging large segments of the general public in serious discussion of public policy issues."[5] The consortium's plans were ambitious—a national support system, a headquarters, and a clearinghouse for study circles. It wanted "to spread the concept of study circles as a learning tool, . . . produce directories and handbooks, . . . establish regional centers to form local study circles, and train facilitators in New York State and then across the nation."[6]

It was able to launch "parenting circles" on parent education through the New York State Education Department, several firms adopted the study circle idea, and the consortium introduced study circles around the state. But it could not extend the idea of study circles beyond New York State, mainly because (1) study circles did not generate enough participation or revenue to make their establishment profitable for adult and continuing education programs; (2) the consortium failed to find organizational bases to institutionalize the format; and (3) study circles were perceived as just another adult education methodology in search of substance, or program content.

Still, Kurland's New York State Consortium constitutes the only place in the United States where a systematic effort was made to introduce study circles into existing practice, up to their introduction to a national issues discussion program, the Domestic Policy Association's National Issues Forums, and to a major union, the International Union of Bricklayers and Allied Craftsmen. These two programs are presented as case studies in the following chapter.

7

. . . .

Study Circles
In the United States

The following two examples of study circle adoption illustrate how the Swedish study circle model can be transplanted to another culture. Both examples are based in popular movements, one newly created and the other already existing in trade union membership. Both started with the organization's program content; both derive their legitimacy from their members and constituencies; and both borrow their pedagogy and terminology, adapted for American practice, from the Swedish study circle experience.

CASE STUDY 1

The Domestic Policy Association's National Issues Forums

The newest national program in the United States to further the goals of adult civic education is the National Issues Forums (NIF), sponsored by the Domestic Policy Association (DPA) in Dayton, Ohio. The DPA/NIF seeks ways to bring citizens (and advanced high school students) into the policy-making processes in the belief that informed citizens can affect the way the public considers and acts on issues touching our lives and our communities.

As David Mathews, president of the Kettering Foundation, DPA/NIF's primary initial sponsor, put it in *National Forum*, the basic test of a democracy "is the relation of the people to their government." Mathews goes on to talk about "popular sovereignty"—informed citizens taking part in and shaping public life, holding and expressing strong values and judgments, challenging policymakers with facts and ideas, and gaining vitality from sharing varied interests and views to determine their common stake in public issues.[1]

In attempting to carry out this mission, the DPA/NIF has essentially created a grass-roots, community-based movement of organizations and institutions (libraries, senior centers, civic associations, community colleges, continuing education divisions, churches) interested in a more informed civic life and in keeping public representatives accountable to the public.

The DPA/NIF began in 1981 faced with a multitude of competing forms of political education—television and radio, newspapers and other print materials, local clubs and civic organizations, university and college continuing education and community service programs, book discussion clubs, public hearings, and ad hoc neighborhood task forces to meet specific issues, to name a few. The United States has a highly educated population, which prides itself on being "informed" and responsive to public issues and on valuing the rights of citizenship.

But slightly over half of us go to the polls for national elections, even fewer for local and state elections. We consistently rank congressmen and other public officials low in our polls of who we believe are trustworthy and who we hold in high respect. Only one in three of us reads a book a year. Only a small percentage of us devotes time to organizing or participating in adult civic education programs—even when the opportunities are available. We have a "glut of information" from many sources, and many of us derive our information and our opinions about public affairs from the nightly television news programs. Our "right to indifference" about public affairs is a cherished American liberty.

We are not a true popular democracy. In fact, despite their rhetoric on the necessity for an educated citizenry, the founding fathers were highly suspicious of the masses participating in any substantial way in public life. And today, most of us are not concerned with enhancing such participation, or even with increasing citizen understanding of public issues. We believe we can confront the bureaucracy by writing a letter, exerting congressional pressure, or airing our grievance in court. Or we believe in the voting booth, where we can always "vote the rascals out." But we would just as soon leave decisions about complex public issues to those who have the knowledge or expertise to make them. For this purpose, we have a republican form of government in which we elect representatives who, along with nonelected public officials, are charged with making the right decisions about our nation's future. We expect these decisions to be made based on concepts of equality and justice reflecting basic values and the public's interests rather than interests that appeal to an articulate and aggressive few seeking special privileges.

But it doesn't always happen this way, and there is growing public clamor for more citizen involvement in decision making. If we look at the history of public forum movements in the United States, however, we know that most suffer a demise after a few years when their sponsorship or funding is withdrawn. We simply have no counterpart to the ninety-year experience of the Swedish study circle movement.

When it was launched in 1981, the DPA/NIF had fourteen national organizations and foundations interested in building a decentralized nationwide program to enable citizens to use public issue discussion to bridge the gap between citizen and policymaker, to offer informed citizen views on important national issues, and to provide policymakers with "political permission" to make public policy decisions. In the fall of 1982, these initial organizations developed twenty local public forum programs, which took on three major national issues, and the DPA/NIF has grown every year since. It just completed its fifth operational year in fall 1986 and reports local community forums in over two hundred communities in almost every state reaching some one hundred thousand adults in total. The local sponsors include a wide range of educational, civic, and voluntary organizations.

The national DPA/NIF is a voluntary, nonprofit, nonpartisan network of organizations interested in public issue discussion. The program is open to any community organization that wants to develop community forums, and there are no rigid requirements for conducting these forums. The materials, developed by the Public Agenda Foundation in New York, are high quality and include well-illustrated, readable issue books along with video and audio "starting tapes" on the three issues chosen by the local conveners for discussion each fall. The books and tapes clearly delineate the spectrum of choices we as citizens face on important policy issues, and the consequences and trade-offs inherent in each choice.

The community forums use a distinct methodology that encourages participants to "work through" issues in open discussion by airing differences, confronting diverse opinions, and moving from initial opinions and positions to second and third opinions during the course of the discussions. Training for forum conveners and moderators is essential to the "working-through" concept and the effectiveness of the group discussions. The forums close their programs when participants complete opinion questionnaires on each issue. The hoped-for result is collective "public judgment" on the issue (as opposed to "public opinion," the result of public opinion polling), which is then shared with local and national policymakers through a variety of reporting-back mechanisms that include a national teleconference, an annual citizens-policymakers' conference held at one of the presidential libraries, and "Washington Week" when forum representatives present their findings to Washington officials. Policymakers are also increasingly participating in the local forums.

Besides its success in developing a widespread, public-oriented discussion program in its first several years of operation, the DPA/NIF program has taken root in local communities. This is because of its decentralized nature, its flexibility and tolerance of local diversity, and the unique opportunity it offers for everyday citizens to have their voices heard and opinions registered in the corridors of power and decision making. But within the local communities, it has tended to go for numbers, adapting traditional formats of one-time public lectures, well-known speakers to draw audiences, expert panels, and audience discussion. Sometimes these larger audiences are broken down into smaller discussion groups, which report their findings to the plenary.

Most local conveners use steering committees and extensive publicity channels in seeking audiences for their forums. In its first few years, DPA/NIF program organizers often heard a local convener apologetically comment, "I expected 250 people and only 60 showed up for our forum!" Many conveners overestimated the drawing power of public forums; the competition for the public's time is often fierce and overwhelming. More significantly, their expectations tended to be in size of audiences; the quality of dialogue—the working-through that can only occur when everyone has an opportunity to participate—was secondary. What an individual participant had to offer and take away from the give-and-take of open exchange of issues had been blurred in the search for large audiences. Forgotten was that true dialogue can only take place in face-to-face settings where, as in the Swedish study circles, all participants are treated as political equals with an equal voice in the procedures, the deliberations, and the outcomes.

Whenever I briefed the Swedish officials on the DPA/NIF program, they were invariably attracted by how DPA brings local conveners into the process of issue selection through the annual balloting, and provides objective, seemingly balanced choices in the issue books. All this stands in direct contrast to the policy of most of the Swedish national educational associations, which, with a few exceptions, like to make their position on public issues known in their study circle materials. The Swedes were also taken with DPA/NIF's efforts to communicate the results of the annual local forums to local and national policymakers. This reporting back only takes place in Sweden when, for

example, the SAP receives questionnaires and letters
from participants in their Idéforums, or when the nation holds a national referendum following study circle
discussions, as it did in 1980 on the nuclear question.
But the Swedes were also curious about the formats
for local discussions, including the use of television,
and asked why study circles wouldn't be appropriate
in spurring on issue discussion in the DPA/NIF network. If they worked in Sweden to further popular
democracy, why wouldn't they work here—especially
since our philosophy was oriented to spirited, critical
public dialogue on major issues through democratic,
community-centered forums. Why shouldn't the
forums themselves be participant centered?

They had a point, and since local DPA/NIF conveners seemed receptive, we introduced the study circle
idea into the literature and methodology of DPA/NIF
in April 1985, prior to the fall 1985 NIF series. Thus,
DPA published a step-by-step guide, *The Study Circle
in the National Issues Forum,*[2] and circulated it to all
actual and potential conveners. Organizers also introduced the concept at DPA's regional training/orienta-
tion for forum leadership.

Most DPA/NIF conveners immediately took to the
study circle as an alternative to large budgets, broad
publicity efforts to attract audiences, keynote speakers, and expert panels. As a complement to larger
forums, it would enable local conveners to reach into
neighborhood organizations, senior centers, and libraries, for example, all of which have limited budgets
and resources for developing large public forums. The
study circle was not to replace the large public forum,
however; it was simply an alternative format to be
geared to local circumstances.

Integrating study circles in the DPA/NIF program

relates philosophically to the working-through methodology to obtain, in Daniel Yankelovich's words, "public judgment on issues [which] cannot be assumed to preexist." Yankelovich compares such informed public judgment—that is, collective judgments arising from open, spirited citizen dialogue—with "mass opinion" as measured by public opinion polls and the "vagaries of the public viewpoint at a moment in time." For Yankelovich, "public judgment reflects the public's viewpoint once people have had an opportunity to confront an issue seriously and over an extended period of time."[3] Study circles, in contrast to one-shot large-event public forums, offer sustained, serious study and discussion of public issues, enhancing the potential for the working-through process to occur.

DPA recently solicited seven case studies and conducted a national survey of veteran conveners. The issues that were addressed were the fall 1985 NIF topics of taxation, welfare, and relationships with the Soviets. The resulting "Reports from the Field" showed that three basic models are used for local forum programs.[4] One of these models relies on study circles as the primary instrument for citizen discussion of issues, and another uses them in collaboration with larger gatherings.

In Model 1, the citywide DPA/NIF Steering Committee promotes and conducts large public forums, one on each issue, in accessible public halls and employs speakers, expert panelists, small group discussion during the sessions, and group reports.

In Model 2, the citywide Steering Committee encourages each of its member organizations to conduct study circles for its members and constituencies, and then submits the study circle results to a citywide "reporting-back" forum with policymakers.

Model 3 has a lead community institution (a community college, a library, a university), which devotes substantial resources, often in collaboration with other institutions, for a series of forums and study circles on the issues.

In a follow-up survey to veteran conveners, DPA found they used a variety of formats—large forums, small group discussions within larger forums, study circles, television panels, and reporting-back forums, often used in combination—in their DPA/NIF programs. A majority also reported moving toward greater use of small group discussion, especially study circles, to encourage participants to read the issue books, to facilitate informal discussion, and to enhance the working-through process. Their study circles usually met for an average of three sessions per issue, attracting ten to twelve participants and using trained study circle leaders (moderators). Most conveners wanted to have more sessions and to find ways to train their leaders more effectively. Some program examples follow.

In Tucson, Arizona, the NIF encouraged neighborhood study circles in the fall 1985 series. These circles were sponsored by thirty community organizations—libraries, Native American and Mexican-American neighborhood organizations, colleges, civic associations, the League of Women Voters, senior centers, and community centers. Representatives from neighborhood study circles attended citywide forums to report back their results to local and national policymakers. Tucson also experimented with live, two-way cable TV on the three issues with local study circles performing as "listening posts," calling in their questions and comments.

Anita Fonte, Tucson NIF director, likes the blend

of process and content that the study circles afford. She believes "more time needs to be spent in study circle discussion," observing that "the role of issue experts or policymakers is shifting from lecturer to participant and listener," and that "citizens who have participated need a sense of closure."[5] Fonte's program continued in fall 1986 with study circles meeting at the library and its branches, at the Historical Society, and culminating in "town hall meetings" on each of the three DPA/NIF issues.

In Grand Rapids, Michigan, another veteran NIF convener, retired businessman Carl Eschels, reported that in his 1985 NIF program, four convening organizations (Senior Neighbors, Urban League Guild, Friends of the Library, and Grand Rapids Junior College) sponsored eight study circles for 196 citizens on the DPA/NIF issues. After the organizational study circles met, representatives came together in a citywide reporting-back forum involving the district's congressman, a state senator, a county commissioner, and the Grand Rapids city manager. For his 1986 NIF series, Eschels expanded his study circle program to nine organizational sponsors, each study circle meeting for several sessions on the fall 1986 series' topics, with fifteen to twenty participants in each study circle. "The result of using the study circle format," he says, "is better informed participants." According to Eschels:

> The study circle format helped us to overcome two obstacles from the prior year—not enough advance preparation and not enough time for discussion. . . . By concentrating more on quality discussion than quantity, i.e., number of participants, . . . we enhanced our NIF program immeasurably. The study circle format is the way to

go whenever you have a group of citizens who can
meet on a regular basis.[6]

John Buskey, associate dean of continuing education,
University of Nebraska at Lincoln, reported four pilot
study circles in fall 1985 for forty-eight participants
meeting in five two-hour sessions. They too focused
on taxes (two study circles), welfare (one study circle),
and the Soviets (one study circle). Buskey describes
his program:

> Each study circle's initial meeting served as an
> orientation, during which participants received
> the issue book, viewed the videotapes, and dis-
> cussed outside resources on the topic. During
> subsequent meetings, circle members discussed
> the issues, led by University faculty who served
> as moderators. Careful training helped the mod-
> erators avoid certain pitfalls. . . . If the moderators
> happened to be experts on a particular topic, the
> circle members tended to want a lecture on the
> subject, . . . but we encouraged the moderators to
> focus talk on the discussion guide questions
> rather than turn the forum into a classroom.[7]

Finally, convener Ray Gildea, associate director of
the Stennis Institute of Government at Mississippi
State University, reports that the Starkville, Mississippi, NIF used study circles to focus community attention on the welfare issue and to come up with recommendations for the county. The program included a
four-week series of noontime, brown-bag study circles,
which brought local welfare experts, case workers,
and welfare recipients together to discuss the government's role in welfare, alternatives to welfare, and
public and private sources of funding. Gildea reported

that the most significant action produced by the study circles was a proposal to establish a local Human Resources Council, an umbrella group to improve communications among various agencies working on the welfare issue.

After the pilot study circles were introduced to the DPA/NIF network in 1985, convener acceptance steadily increased to the point that, for the fall 1986 NIF series on crime, the farm crisis, and immigration, approximately one-third of the conveners used study circles in their forum programs. The circles were often held in conjunction with television broadcasts and reporting-back forums with policymakers.

For example, in its first experience with the NIF program, the San Jose Public Library held afternoon and evening study circles—two sessions for each of the three issues—in the main library and three branch libraries for over one hundred participants. The University of Maine Cooperative Extension Service, Franklin County Office (Farmington), selected the NIF program to increase the leadership ability of involved individuals and to inform the general public of important policy issues; the office conducted study circles throughout the county prior to holding a countywide forum on the issues at the University of Maine campus. And Wright State University's Center for Economic Education in Dayton, Ohio, conducted a study circle on the crime issue in a noontime session at a senior center, and held others at the main library and branch libraries, churches, a community college, the University of Dayton, and Wright State University.

Other examples drawn from the 1986 DPA/NIF program include study circles on the farm crisis in Pine River, Minnesota, sponsored by the Minnesota DPA; community study circles preceding major forums on each issue and sponsored by the NIF-Iowa City Steering Committee operating out of the University of Iowa's Division of Continuing Education and by thirteen cosponsoring organizations; the Port Washington (New York) Free School District's Community Education Program, which held study circles for its adult literacy students using special editions of the NIF issue books; and study circles in the farm community of Dubuque, Iowa, sponsored by Continuing Education at the University of Dubuque, held in churches, colleges, and county extension offices, and resulting in a countywide forum on the farm crisis issue.

Even though DPA/NIF's experience with study circles is limited, we can detect some convener enthusiasm among those seeking an alternative to large forums and sizable allocation of institutional resources to the NIF program. Whenever the study circle idea has been tried, the public has responded. Whether because of our history of coming together or our desire to be heard in public affairs, conveners reportedly are not having difficulty attracting study circle participants, and the previous disappointment with lower-than-anticipated audiences has been largely muted.

Senior centers, libraries, community college and university continuing education divisions, and other institutions with limited resources and a "pay-as-you-go" policy can easily develop study circles and thereby participate in the national program. The study circle has enabled these conveners to reach out to neighborhood audiences—to people unaccustomed to large citywide forums, especially minority groups—and to bring them into the policy-making process.

Inexpensiveness, ease of promotion, ease in finding meeting sites, encouragement of face-to-face discussion and working-through issues—all seem to be key

factors in the acceptance of study circles as an effective
public issue discussion format for the DPA/NIF. When
used in conjunction with larger, reporting-back
forums—as in Tucson, Grand Rapids, Iowa City, and
other sites—the study circle can be instrumental in
providing in-depth judgments on the issues, which can
then be shared with policymakers.

There is no model study circle universally adopted
by the DPA/NIF network, but all meet for more than
one session, use both video and print materials, and
employ trained moderators. It is too early to state that
new DPA/NIF leadership is emerging from the local
study circles, or that study circles are active in other
community affairs, or that participants are using the
process in other programs—all outcomes documented
in the Swedish study circle experience—but these are
areas for future analysis.

Jon Rye Kinghorn, national coordinator of DPA,
believes strongly in the efficacy of the study circle
approach for the DPA/NIF network, especially when
it is complemented by large citywide or regional
forums. In a recent conversation, Kinghorn observed
that "we want to keep our ideas coming from the grass
roots up, and study circles seem an ideal vehicle to
accomplish this purpose."

We are indeed an "information society," with a
strong and growing citizen urge to understand civic
life, to participate more directly in public affairs, to
be heard, and to communicate our views to people who
make decisions that affect our lives. After all, for a
nation that believes in having informed, critical, and
civically responsible citizens to keep government accountable, ideas and information necessary to decide
public issues must be shared with the public if power
is to be shared as well. That is DPA/NIF's purpose,

and as this popular movement for an increasingly informed and active citizenry expands over the next few
years, study circles promise to become a vital force
for small-scale democracy within the larger DPA/NIF
program.

CASE STUDY 2

The Bricklayers and Allied Craftsmen's
Study Circle Program

In the summer of 1986, the International Union (IU)
of Bricklayers and Allied Craftsmen (BAC) conducted
twenty-seven experimental pilot study circles on the
future of the union and the masonry industry. The
response was extraordinary. Led by IU field staff and
business agents, the circles attracted approximately
270 local union officers and rank-and-file members from
fourteen states and two Canadian provinces. Participants discussed in depth the final report of the BAC's
Project 2000 Committee, which had deliberated over
eighteen months on the enormous problems faced by
the union and on alternatives for the future.

The previous year, President John T. Joyce and the
BAC Executive Board, after presenting the committee's report to IU's 1985 Convention, had been searching for ways to bring the members into the discussion.
The study circle format, used successfully for years
by the Swedish trade union movement, seemed an appropriate vehicle to inform the members about Project
2000 and to elicit their informed opinions about the
findings and recommendations.

Two forces came together in mid-1985 that would
influence the development of the BAC Study Circle
Program.

The thirty-six member Project 2000 Committee,

composed of U.S. and Canadian business agents, had met from mid-1983 until summer 1985 in intensive discussions of the union's problems, structure, and future. One of the committee's proposals was for a unionwide member education program to get members' views on the union's future. "All BAC members should have the chance to go through a similar process," stated the 1985 report, "as only the members of the BAC can make the final determination of what their Union should be."[8]

At this time, President Joyce, having had a hand in the AFL-CIO's well-received, influential report, "The Changing Situation of Workers and Their Unions" (1985), which called for increased member participation in their unions and in discussion of union issues and of broader social issues, was looking for an appropriate mode of worker education that could lay the foundation for an expanded BAC education program.

The BAC, like most building trades unions, did not have a history of strong member education programs; however, it had the obvious advantage of starting fresh, and it had a built-in content with the Project 2000 Committee's report, in which the committee had called on the IU "to establish an educational program with 'study circles' as a basic component." The report continues:

> Patterned after a highly successful effort in Sweden, and drawing on lessons learned from a pilot "study circle" effort involving a local BAC union, this type of program is designed to enable BAC members and their families to meet in small groups and . . . discuss a broad range of issues affecting them and the union.[9]

The BAC's convention in September 1985 endorsed

the committee report and the study circle pilot series, after which the IU started planning for the 1986 summer series. It would be the first international union in North America to adopt the Swedish study circle model.

From the start, the IU wanted to learn from the pilot study circles and looked upon them as the forerunners for an expanded BAC education program. The pilot study circles would be planned for both business agents and rank-and-file members, and the Project 2000 Report would serve as the core content.

Borrowing heavily from the Swedish trade union experience with study circles, BAC defined its study circles as "voluntary, highly participatory, and democratic." Offered free to members and their families, each study circle would have a minimum of five members and a maximum of twenty, and would meet weekly for five weeks in 2½-hour sessions for a total of 12½ hours. Study circle organizers would take responsibility for recruiting participants, making local arrangements, obtaining materials, and reporting results; study circle leaders would actually lead the discussion sessions. Organizers and leaders would be drawn from the fifteen IU field staff and the thirty-six business agent members of the Project 2000 Committee.

Study circles would be planned for business agents from a region or state; for business agents and other local officers in a local area; and for rank-and-file members from a single local. The materials would be derived from the Project 2000 Report and would include an introductory brochure, an *Organizer's Handbook*, issue booklets on major sections of the Project 2000 Report, an introductory ten-minute video entitled "Shaping the Future," *Leader's Guides* for each session, and supplementary handouts. Finally, all organizers, leaders, and participants would receive attractive certificates on completion of the program.

President Joyce outlined the IU objectives for the BAC Study Circle Program in a January 1986 letter in which he informed IU field staff and Project 2000 Committee members about their upcoming role in the pilot series:

> To build member understanding of the Project 2000 Committee's recommendations, and obtain members' views on how the recommendations might affect the locals, the future of our union, and the masonry industry.
>
> To raise the morale and sense of pride and well-being of our members, their families, and our retirees through open, candid discussion and increased participation in the union and in their communities.
>
> To develop an effective communications mechanism for involving locals and their members in the life of the union, and for increasing cooperation with other locals and with organizations important to BAC's future.

The topics for the five scheduled study circle sessions, presented in attractive, readable, and well-illustrated issue booklets, emphasized the choices and trade-offs faced by the BAC in the years ahead:

> SESSION 1
> *"Where We Stand: Challenges to Our Jobs and Our Union"*
> Designed to get the discussion started by examining the status of the union, the job picture, what the union does, and what the union should be.

SESSION 2

"The Masonry Industry Today"
Problems in the industry, the union's relationship
with the industry, and what needs to be done.

SESSION 3

"The Broader Context"
An in-depth analysis of the forces affecting the
union—in the labor movement, the government,
the business community, and the general public—
and BAC relationships with these sectors.

SESSION 4

"What We Can Do: Building a Stronger Industry"
The Project 2000 program proposals for masonry
industry revival through advertising and promotion, research and development, and masonry
craft training—and how to pay for these programs.

SESSION 5

"What We Can Do: Building a Stronger Union"
Proposals for union reorganization, including
regionalization, effective financial management,
expanded membership services, organizing,
collective bargaining, and political action.

The goals for this first series of pilot study circles
were predictably modest, with twelve to fifteen study
circles anticipated. As the program's introductory
brochure, "A Look at Project 2000," points out:

the relatively few study circles planned for 1986
cannot change the way a union, or any organization is run. But operating over time, a large number of study circles, with informed and participating members, will make that organization
better. Increased identification with the union's
concerns and programs, and increased participation can renew vitality in both the union and the
trade union movement.

The IU emphasized from the beginning of the pilot series that the study circles would not be typical union business meetings, with fixed agendas, parliamentary procedure, and majority votes. This meant, however, that the IU field staff and Project 2000 Committee business agents leading the study circles would have to be trained for the new role.

Two training sessions were held—in Bal Harbour, Florida, in February 1986 and in Annapolis, Maryland, in May 1986. Enthusiasm among participants ran high at the initial training session, with a general "Let's try it" attitude. The officers saw in the BAC Study Circle Program an opportunity to link Project 2000's call for member involvement with a new educational format for the union. They observed that the Project 2000 Committee itself was an extended study circle and that the program was timely.

Between the Bal Harbour and Annapolis training sessions, BAC's *Journal,* the monthly newsletter for the union, highlighted the program ("Study Circles to Provide New Communications Tool") in its February 1986 issue, and IU published a monthly newsletter on the program, the *Study Circle Program Update.*

The Annapolis training included presentation of the program's new introductory video, "Shaping the Future"; explanation on use of the issue booklets; distribution of an "Organizer's Packet" with flyers, sample letters, and forms for scheduling a study circle and ordering materials; and the conduct of an actual study circle with members on Session 1. The study circle reinforced the leader's role of remaining neutral and bringing in all viewpoints while guiding the discussion. The training stressed that the study circle was to be a dialogue, a setting for exchanging and challenging views and finding common ground, and that no majority votes or consensus would be sought. Study circle leaders were encouraged to demonstrate the relationship between the members' personal problems and needs and the larger issues, to review and summarize as the study circle proceeded, and to look upon disagreements as productive and thought-provoking.

By mid-May, over half the IU field staff and Project 2000 Committee members had committed themselves to organizing and leading a study circle. As one western business agent exclaimed, "We've got to start listening to the members—I'm all for it."

By early June, ten BAC study circles were in operation. George Shuman, IU special deputy in Jacksonville, Florida, had jumped the gun and conducted the first study circle on 8 May for eight Florida business agents at the union's state conference. "It turned into an old-fashioned union meeting," he reported. "We used the issue booklet, . . . everyone participated, we respected each other's opinions, and the agents came up with good suggestions." A good start!

By mid-July, the IU knew it would have at least twenty-five study circles, possibly more, in both the United States and Canada. Most circles reported taking on all five issues, one per week in the union hall or local hotel, alleviating initial union fears that it would be difficult to sustain an extended summer series. Time and travel distances did restrict some study circles to three sessions, however, and a few took on all five issues in a weekend "conference-style" format.

The study circles took place in large locals and in smaller locals, in bricklayers' locals, in tile-setters' locals, and in multicraft locals. They were conducted in large cities and small towns, in areas for high employment for masonry craftsmen and in pockets of high unemployment. The members responded positively to the opportunity to voice their opinions and share ideas on the future of their union.

Early reports of these first study circle sessions were gratifying. Members attended, and recruitment did not seem to be a problem. Discussions were substantive and serious, showing the depth of member concern for their jobs and their union. No longer a concept borrowed from Swedish trade union experiences, the BAC Study Circle Program was beginning to take root, and the BAC was developing its own models. Attendance for the five sessions held steady, with little attrition, and members participated with a vitality and enthusiasm surprising even to their study circle leaders.

The IU had obviously struck a resonant chord with this new educational format. Dominic Spano, IU special deputy from Albany, and Andrew Gallante, business agent for Local 44 in Poughkeepsie, talked about their joint study circle for sixteen upstate New York business agents: "We went the full two hours without a single hitch and covered every item in the Session 1 issue booklet. The guys were serious. Everyone had a chance to talk. It went well."

Charles Dingle, business agent for Local 1 in Charleston, South Carolina, the oldest local in the state, said, "We had twelve journeymen and two apprentices. The men read the booklets for thirty minutes, and then we got into the discussion. The older men talked about what their union was like—'At one time there wasn't a nonunion man working the trade here'—and you could see the younger guys taking it in." Ed Fry, business agent for Local 55 in Columbus, Ohio, a large multicraft local, wanted "to get beyond my friends, or else it's no challenge." He reported on recruiting study circle participants: "I just told them that it is your

union, and if you want to be a part of it, you'll want
to participate. Nine guys signed up after the meeting."
Anecdotes from the sessions were starting to come in.
Knowing that the BAC pilot study circle series was
a first for the U.S. and Canadian trade union movements, the IU wanted to gather as much information
as possible on the pilot series before deciding on the
future of the program, and to communicate the results
to other trade unions and labor organizations. Data-
gathering techniques included telephone and written
reports from the study circle leaders following each
session; site visits to study circle sessions; videotaping
of selected study circle sessions; participant questionnaires completed after Session 5 and final leader questionnaires; and oral reports and videos at the Project
2000 Committee's meeting in Chicago on 4 August and
at the IU's Local Officers' Seminar at Notre Dame on
14 October 1986.

IU field staff and Project 2000 Committee members
met in Chicago, 4–5 August 1986, and the meeting
offered the first opportunity for the union to hear the
anecdotes and insights from the pilot study circles:

> "There was so much to discuss in Session 3 ("The
> Broader Context") that we forgot the time—I
> couldn't turn them off."
>
> > Ed Fry, Local 55
> > Columbus, Ohio

> "There's always the danger that the study circle
> will turn into a rap session, with guys just taking
> off and talking. So I stayed with the *Leader's
> Guide,* asked questions to guide the discussion,
> and the men responded."
>
> > Mike Aquiline
> > IU vice president
> > Pittsburgh, Penn.

"Our group met at the Union Hall for over two hours. In fact, I had to call it a night to get them to break up. . . . It was reminiscent of the first meetings of Project 2000."

Robert Ritchie, Local 6
Fort Worth, Texas

"Some of our guys came with simplistic views, but after our discussion, realized how complex the problems are."

Ray Allen, Local 1
Oklahoma City, Okla.

These preliminary oral reports from the study circle leaders enabled the IU to reach some tentative conclusions about the Study Circle Program:

Recruiting of study circle participants did not appear to be a major problem.

The study circles for business agents tended to become "policy circles" as the business agents seemed generally aware of the issues.

The materials (both video and print) were crucial to the success of these first study circles, with leaders following them religiously.

The study circle leader, whether IU field staff or business agent, was out of his usual role—"It was not a normal business meeting," said one, and all seemed cognizant of the need to stay neutral to let the discussions flow.

It was obvious from the enthusiasm displayed in the initial reports that the program was working, even for summer sessions, with many sessions running over the allotted time.

By the time of the Local Officers' Seminar held for

250 business agents and other local officials at Notre Dame, 13–15 October 1986, the pilot series had been completed. One full session was turned over to the leaders' reporting on the study circle results, along with videotaped excerpts from several study circles in action.

The mood at the Notre Dame Seminar was upbeat. The BAC Study Circle Program had accomplished what it had set out to do—to bring back some pride in the union, to involve members in open discussion of issues faced by the union and the masonry industry, and to create a format for an expanded member education program. The reports dramatically illustrated that BAC officers and rank-and-file members are deeply concerned about their union, want to talk about the issues the union faces, and want their opinions heard. There were also some unanticipated dividends.

For example, in his final written report on his study circle, Ben Fleming, IU special deputy from British Columbia, reported that he had reached fifteen Canadian and U.S. business agents in the northwest and that it was the first time the Canadians and Americans could talk at such length and in such candor about their mutual problems. He also cited the study circle as the catalyst for helping settle a tricky, intraunion dispute among several locals.

Val Anderson, business agent for Local 18 in Los Angeles, said in his report that his members "were much more aware of the double-breasting problem after the study circle and agreed to report any instances of it." Noble Cain, IU vice president in Illinois, reported on one member who had always been quiet, "but after the study circle, which honestly valued his opinion, he said he wanted to be more active in the local and might even run for office."

"We came to realize," said Trygve Espeland, business manager for Local 56 in Carol Stream, Illinois, in summarizing his experience, "that the only common denominator in the masonry industry is the skilled craftsman, contributing his or her skill and money to boost the industry. It is only logical that the BAC be the catalyst to . . . provide the direction and leadership to maximize the industry's potential." And William Christopher, IU vice president from New Orleans, echoed a common sentiment in his assessment: "Now that the word is out about the BAC's study circles, I'm finding more and more men who want to join."

The pilot series, however, was not problem free. Summer scheduling, when bricklayers and other masonry craftsmen are fully employed, played havoc with several of the five-week study circles. More "outside experts" and guests might have brought greater depth to some of the discussions. Sessions tended to run over the scheduled times, and leaders occasionally found it difficult to keep their participants focused on the issues. Some participants had not read the issue booklets and had trouble keeping up with the others, although this problem was usually resolved after the first session as members got into the habit of reading the booklets in advance. Several leaders reported their study circles slow in starting but picking up as the members became accustomed to the give-and-take format. Guy Mizer, secretary-treasurer of Local 3 in Phoenix, Arizona, observed in a telephone conversation that "it improved as we went along as they paid more attention to the topic—looking at the issue rather than griping or trying to assign blame for our problems."

Following the Notre Dame reporting session, enthusiasm for the study circle concept was running high, with several nonparticipating officers asking how they

could conduct a study circle or even being more specific:
"I'm concerned about health and welfare benefits—
could I get a study circle started with my members?"
But it was the study circle leader who offered the most
dramatic testimony in the final report on the program:[10]

> "The business agent from Tucson Local 1 drove to
> Phoenix weekly for all five sessions."
>
> > C. Wayne Carpenter
> > IU special deputy
> > Tulsa, Okla.

> "Members praised the BAC for trying to shape a
> better future, to save our jobs and our union, and
> the masonry industry. . . . The guys want to be
> involved. There was better participation than I
> expected."
>
> > Jean Guindon, Local 4
> > Montreal

> "The only problem I had in Session 3 was cutting
> off discussion. We didn't need outside experts for
> this one—these guys are the experts. . . . Our
> study circle has created an enthusiastic mood
> among the participants; most have indicated they
> will conduct their own study circles."
>
> > Ben Fleming
> > IU special deputy
> > British Columbia

> "We created interest in union matters which are
> causing problems for all trades. We all realize
> something must be done soon or we face loss of
> jobs. . . . We have a few new leaders for our next
> study circle program. We enjoyed it."
>
> > Hubert Stockhausen
> > Local 2
> > Washington, D.C.

"The group felt that the study circle has been real beneficial to them in understanding the overall issues that face the union. They suggest that all locals should hold these types of meetings as a way to better inform the membership."

Ray Allen, Local 1
Oklahoma City, Okla.

"The five study circle sessions were of value beyond my expectations. It was a learning process for me as well as the participants. We plan to continue on a quarterly basis in Ventura County as well as Orange County. The IU has undertaken a program that has great potential and it couldn't come at a better time. The membership wants to be involved."

William Armstrong
Local 18
Los Angeles, Calif.

Study circle participants were asked to complete a survey questionnaire after their study circle program, and seventy-two questionnaires (27 percent) were returned. Reports indicate that 115 officers and 155 local members attended the study circles. A prototypical study circle had eight to twelve members who met for five weekly sessions, usually in the evening, at the union office or hall (57 percent), at a hotel or restaurant (23 percent), or in a private home (14 percent). The survey showed that older members, aged 45–64, made up 67 percent of the participants, followed by 24 percent aged 30–44, which meant that the experienced members were attending.

Few study circles reported difficulty in recruiting participants. Most heard about the study circle at a union meeting (44 percent), through personal contact

(36 percent), or from Project 2000 (14 percent). Only 5 percent were reached by flyers, posters, letters, or other printed materials. Most participants joined the study circle because they thought it was their responsibility as a union member (27 percent), because they wanted to learn more (16 percent), or because they wanted to let the union know their opinions (18 percent). Some (19 percent) were asked to join by a union officer, some (12 percent) liked the idea of small group discussion, and some (5 percent) wanted to get together with other union members. As one respondent put it, "I was simply curious about how it would work."

Finally, 93 percent of the participants attended from three to five sessions, and their comments were highly supportive: "Informative," "interesting," "good idea," "educational and enlightening," "great discussions," and "good exchange of ideas and points of view." Others simply wanted to learn and let others hear their views—"I got my two cents worth in—it is important to let people know your opinions," or "I learned something and got to express my views—views that might not come out at a regular business meeting."

The BAC Study Circle Program distributed a range of video and print materials for the 1986 pilot series, and almost all participants found them "informative" and "well put together," and said "they helped to get the discussion going." They "got me thinking," said one local member in a typical comment, "and were the basis for our discussions." Another participant, a local officer, observed: "The booklets brought up subjects that your average member wouldn't really think about." Some 80 percent of the participants had read at least three of the five issue booklets in advance, and 40 percent had read all five—both percentages high for a program of this nature. Almost 50 percent wanted more video, and a number requested "more localized materials."

In their response to the question about the quality of their discussions, participants responded overwhelmingly (83 percent) that their study circle had "open give-and-take discussion where everybody had an opportunity to present his views." Only 11 percent felt there was just "some open discussion," and 6 percent thought there was "little open discussion—one or a few participants dominated throughout." Among their comments:

> "Some new ideas came out and most of the members were able to voice their frustrations and have their concerns addressed."

> "Nobody was afraid to voice his opinion."

> "No one in our study circle was bashful."

> "Everyone had an opportunity to improve his mind."

> "Friendly and informed—the atmosphere provided for a free expression of ideas."

Even though BAC study circle leaders were encouraged to bring in outside experts on the participants' terms, only 25 percent reported having guests in their sessions. Almost 50 percent of the participants wanted more outsiders. As one business agent said, "I realized too late that it would have been beneficial to have had outside guests—politicians, labor leaders, architects and engineers, educators, and the like." As they become more comfortable with the format, however, circle leaders will probably be calling in more outside experts on specific topics.

Almost all the study circles met for the full 2½ hours

per session; 90 percent of the participants reported having sufficient time in their discussions although some discussions ran over at the members' choice. The weekend study circles, which permitted only 1¹/₂ hours per session, were reportedly short on time for all sessions. In a typical statement, one member reported, "Our discussions usually continued afterward in the parking lot," and another said, "There was so much interest we could have talked all night."

When asked how effective the study circle format was as a means of member education, 14 percent considered their study circle "outstanding," and 13 percent labeled it only "fair" (some sessions were good, others not so productive), whereas 75 percent thought they were "generally good." This means that about 89 percent of those responding rated their study circles very high as a means for member education.

The BAC, a "union of locals," had no prior history of widespread, systematic member education, so it was all the more surprising to receive the following types of comments from participants on their study circles:

> "We need more effective ways like this to bring our members together."

> "As a result of the study circle, I plan to arrange a session locally among our members to air their views—they want to talk."

> "Even though some problems were not resolved, I believe everyone left with a much better understanding of the issues."

> "We need more of them—it makes us feel involved in our union."

One member, however, voiced concern: "We feel powerless to affect change." Overcoming this sense of de-

tachment and powerlessness, in addition to examining
issues in depth, may be one of the most important
outcomes for the BAC Study Circle Program.

The testimony offered by the participants indicates
that a sizable majority (56 percent) either "learned a
few things I didn't know" or "feel much better informed
about BAC, the local, the masonry industry." A few
(12 percent) didn't believe they changed their opinions
about the issues, some learned more about study circles
(14 percent), and a handful (7 percent) thought they
would become more involved in union affairs as a result
of participating in a study circle. As one member put
it, "I'm more aware of the need for additional funds,
and I feel better about how the funds will be used."

All the respondents want the study circle program
to continue:

> "The Study Circle Program should be a perma-
> nent educational program."

> "Seems to be a good idea. Keep trying."

> "It's the way to go to make the IU member know
> that his ideas and voice do mean something."

> "Participants in our group gained insights into the
> union that will be beneficial to them and will
> spread to other members."

> "Promote study circles nationally. Get more
> members involved. Good program."

> "Listen to what was said. We are important too."

William Armstrong, business manager for Local 18 in
Los Angeles, led a study circle and summed up the
general feeling about the pilot series when he reported:
"The IU has undertaken a program that has great
potential and it couldn't come at a better time. I hope

it is not put on the back burner as I would like to see us jump in with both feet. From my experience, the membership is anxious to get involved." And Bill Simier, a local member from Opelousas, Louisiana, simply said, "Thank you for asking my opinion on the issues."

The 1986 BAC Study Circle Program, a pilot series to lay the groundwork for a full-fledged union educational program reaching all members, provided the union with insights on how study circles can function in an international union. Over 50 percent of the IU field staff and Project 2000 members volunteered to organize and lead the twenty-seven study circles reaching 270 members in fourteen states and two provinces. The reports from the study circles were overwhelmingly positive, with preliminary results from member polling showing that those who attended the study circles were dramatically more supportive of the union and its plans for the future than were those not attending. The program exceeded the union's expectations, and the leadership plans to expand it in 1987.

Especially encouraging was the extent to which the program successfully met the objectives originally outlined by President Joyce in his 1986 letter:

To build member understanding of the Project 2000 Committee's Report. From the field reports, it was obvious that the study circles provided valuable information about the Project 2000 Report that members probably could not have gotten otherwise. The video and the issue booklets, condensed from the report, proved useful starting points for the discussions, and they were universally popular in laying out the basic issues. There was little attrition, the sessions were serious and informed, and the members want them to continue.

They appreciated having their views shared with IU leadership.

To raise member morale and sense of pride in the union. The study circles were give-and-take discussions on issues affecting the union, with 83 percent of the participants reporting that their study circle offered an opportunity for everyone to present his views. Members were pleased their union had initiated the study circle program, the first in North America, and most saw it as a means to create a stronger, better union through education. The study circle process acknowledges the value of member opinions on union issues, and the effect will undoubtedly carry over to business meetings, other union affairs, and community and political life.

To develop an effective communications mechanism. The Swedish study circles are called "miniature democracies" by their trade union sponsors, and the BAC Study Circle Program reflects this view. Local members, often coming directly from their job sites and at times traveling hundreds of miles, came together in good spirit to talk about their problems, their union, their local, and their industry. The study circles were not typical union business meetings. Because of the insistence on a highly participatory atmosphere and leader neutrality, communications among members took place on a level that couldn't be duplicated by the constraints of a regular business meeting. Several study circles will continue to meet regularly, and other members, having heard of the program, have expressed interest in joining.

For a "union of locals," with great local autonomy and no effective member educational program, the BAC has evolved a simple process for member education, which can be used with a variety of topics and in a variety of settings. The Bricklayers have started a process unique to the North American trade union movement. Study circles worked for trade unions in Sweden, in effect helping the Swedish unions develop the country's unique social democratic society, and BAC has demonstrated that the model can be adopted to another culture, to another trade union movement. President Joyce launched the BAC's pilot study circle program in February 1986 with this charge:

> We are the first union in North America to attempt to adopt the study circle format. Democracy requires an ongoing dialogue between leaders and the people they serve. A modern trade union also has to create mechanisms for a dialogue with its members. This is what the study circles are all about.[11]

8

. . . .

The Future
Of Study Circles
In the United States

Arthur Miller once commented that "a great debate is a nation talking to itself." We are a nation that loves to talk—in our organizations, in our communities. Our history is replete with examples of spontaneous movements designed to bring citizens together in open discussions of the issues they face. Some of these movements lasted only a brief time, others for decades, and some are still around. The DPA/NIF has been around for six years and shows promise of some durability. The BAC, with us for over 120 years, is part of the larger trade union movement. Both have successfully adopted the study circle model to accomplish their respective missions. But more needs to be done before this Swedish adult education model gains full acceptance here as a vehicle for democratic debate, both in communities and in organizations like the trade union.

The study circles worked for a rural, undereducated populace in Sweden at the turn of the century. They worked because they provided the citizen both with power that comes from knowledge and critical analysis, and with opportunities to take leadership roles—often for the first time in their lives. They worked because they served an acute educational need of the Swedish adult public and of the popular movements and organizations that reach the public.

In late twentieth-century America, we get our information about public issues from many sources—television, radio, newspapers, magazines and newsletters, fellow workers, neighbors, family. We are reasonably well educated, and most of us have a good share of self-esteem. We are not hesitant to speak our minds. We all belong to some organization or another; we are a "nation of joiners," as Tocqueville called us, where our opinions are sought. And for the most part, we are taken seriously at the ballot box and in our communications with elected representatives. So why should anyone want to join a study circle?

The answer may lie in our innate desire to come together to discuss issues we have in common, to reinforce our opinions, and perhaps at times to change them. It goes back to our founding, to the early town meetings. We believe in representative government, yet we have a profound and healthy skepticism of authority. We know democracy is inefficient, time consuming, and unwieldy, yet we disdain decisions made without consultation or reference to our concerns. We are a dialoguing people, with respect for other opinions because in the end we know we will not be facing extremes in decision making.

The answer may also lie in what David Mathews has to say about "common judgment," which emerges from the collective inquiry, shared opinions, airing of differences, and consensual shaping of public issues that can come from full consideration of the value choices before us and of the consequences of alternative courses of action. According to Mathews:

> To make policy that is truly public, that is in the larger public interest, people must not only have the facts, but they must know what those facts mean to other people, people different from them. Beyond an understanding of differences, an educated public has to find out what is common to all of the different perspectives on an issue, so it can find a basis for action. It is knowing what interests are shared that educates a public.[1]

Mathews indirectly puts his finger on why the study circle movement has been so critical in Sweden's evolution in less than a century into one of the most mature social democratic nations in the world: it enables a citizen to offer an opinion on a level where it is likely to be heard, and it provides the opportunity to share interests in small group discussion, as we would in friendly conversation, to determine what we have in common with our fellow citizens. And it has ensured these qualities as the basis for action in the public arena where all too often, in Sweden and in the United States, political figures and other policymakers voice the rhetoric of citizen communication but go on to ignore the public's judgment, justify their actions from public opinion polls, and then "sell" their conclusions to the public. If we don't know what others think, if we don't confront each other with ideas, there is no "common judgment." And our silence as citizens is taken as acquiescence to policy decisions others make for us.

The Swedish study circle has served that country well as a systematic but simple format for unleashing the average citizen's capabilities for self-governance.

It could work here as well to help us overcome our complacencies and fears, our sense of powerlessness in public life and in our organizations.

"You have to feel like a player or participant to care," commented Daniel Yankelovich at a spring 1985 conference of citizens and policymakers at the John F. Kennedy Library in Boston, "and most citizens don't feel wanted and with good reason. They aren't asked to participate. If they felt they were being asked, they would participate." Sweden learned this lesson almost ninety years ago, and the late Olof Palme reinforced the notion of adult civic education as integral to Swedish democratic life with this eloquent statement (previously quoted in part):

> Sweden is to a fundamental degree a study circle democracy. It is through study circles that generations have trained themselves in critical analysis so as to be able to reach reasoned decisions in working with one another without abandoning their ideals in the process. It is often in study circles that proposals for changes in society have been first considered.[2]

The Swedes—through the popular movements and the national educational associations, by creating study circles as functioning miniature democracies, by actively recruiting the public to attend their study circles, by taking their citizens' views seriously when they do attend—essentially transformed the economic, political, and social base of their society in just two generations.

No such promise can or should be made for the introduction of study circles into our advanced, technologically based, communications-oriented mass society. But it seems an idea worthy of experimentation—

worthy if only to prove that the individual citizen,
worker, trade union member, parent, neighbor, or
community resident has views that should be heard in
policy-making, provided he or she acquires the information to arrive at an informed opinion, and that democracy can thrive at its most fundamental level:
people talking to people about shared concerns and
finding enough in common to be able to discover a
common basis for action.

The adoption of the study circle model by the DPA's
National Issues Forums and the Bricklayers graphi-
cally demonstrates that we care about the vitality of
our democratic institutions, about democratic participation, and about the quality of our policy-making processes in our communities, our organizations, and our
society.

However, study circles might not work in the United
States, despite the two successes documented in this
work, and several preconditions seem to be essential if
our organizations are to develop a sustained interest in
the study circle model:

A social-philosophical context for study circles. It is not a
question of simply importing a useful and attractive educational format, despite its widespread success in another
culture. Study circles are based on principles of democratic theory, the concept of self-growth through education, and enhancement of individual capacity to participate intelligently in public affairs and organizational life.
The key to study circles, therefore, is not found in a
process of discussion but in what they can contribute to
move us toward a more just society, to relate ideas to
action, and to justify our rhetoric about civic and organizational responsibilities. We should know *why* the idea
is sound as well as *how* it can work.

Institutionalization of the study circle process. Study circles
require an organizational structure, like the Swedish
national educational associations, committed to education; additionally, they need organizers to introduce
them, trained leaders (moderators) to guide them, and
quality materials to make them work. Study circles isolated from these elements are just another small group
format. They cannot be imposed on an organization or
they will be short-lived. They must be perceived as integral to an organization's educational program and useful
to further the organizational mission, and they must be
supported by the organization's leadership. With that
established, study circles have great potential for the
type of intensive, face-to-face discussion that makes
democracy a vital force, that gives public judgment its
validity.

Responsiveness to the adult's need to participate. The
Swedish study circle is based on a simple premise: the
individual's desire to exercise some control over his or
her life, and to overcome ignorance or lack of information and feelings of inadequacy and powerlessness
in the face of complex problems that create barriers
to self-determination. The study circle is a compliment
to the individual; it tells adults they are important
enough to be heard, to have a voice in policy-making.
Thus, it enhances possibilities for adult learning by
encouraging participants to formulate their own ideas
about issues and share them with other members—an
objective seldom reached through large lecture halls,
public hearings stacked with expert testimony, business meetings of unions and other organizations, or
television news broadcasts with two-minute glimpses
into long-standing, complex issues.

A concern for content. The study circle has not caught

the imagination of educators in the United States because it has tended to be promoted as a format isolated from program content and organizational mission. The process becomes more important than the content, as in the "group dynamics" movement of the 1950s and 1960s, another methodological tool in the educator's program-planning repertoire. But it is *not* a panacea, and the issues and content should drive the process. Implementation of the study circle idea divorced from these considerations will not be effective.

The study circle is a tool for study and discussion, for democratic participation, for equality among members, and for encouraging members to become their own experts. It is a powerful vehicle for involving people at a fundamental level in the life of their community or organization. It is a proven and powerful means for adult civic education and organizational democracy.

The Swedes who perfected the modern study circle in this manner understood it as an uncomplicated device to bring undereducated, disenfranchised adults into mainstream public and organizational life. It has grown into a widely accepted practice in this small, homogeneous country for the advancement of popular sovereignty and civic intelligence. Whether the study circle model will work in the United States is still an open question, but the experiences from Sweden, translated and put into action by such organizations as the Domestic Policy Association and the International Union of Bricklayers and Allied Craftsmen, hold out some promise that it will. At present, the study circle remains a goal for those interested in individual and organizational growth to consider in their educational plans.

Study circles can work here. As Senator Albert Gore

(D-Tenn.) stated to a gathering of DPA/NIF citizen representatives in May 1985 at the Capitol:

> What was revolutionary about America, and the idea which led to America, was very simple. It was the realization that our most valuable asset is the brainpower of our people—the revolutionary idea that people at the grassroots level were best able to make decisions about their own destinies.

It is still a revolutionary idea, one that, to paraphrase Jefferson, needs constant attention and renewal. The study circles, epitomizing democracy in action, can help.

NOTES

INTRODUCTION

1. During my first visit, which extended from 23 April to 11 May 1984 and was supported by a Swedish Bicentennial Fellowship award, I visited Stockholm, Ludvika, Lund, and Malmö.
2. Brevskolan, *The Study Circle: A Brief Introduction* (Stockholm: Brevskolan, 1980), pp. 13-14.
3. Ibid., p. 26.
4. Worker's Educational Association (ABF), *Workers' Education in Sweden* (Stockholm: ABF, 1973), p. 1.

CHAPTER 1

1. L.P. Oliver, "Chautauqua and the State Humanities Programs: The Quest for Quality and Audiences," in *The Michigan Connection* (East Lansing, Mich.: Michigan Council for the Humanities, 1984), p. 12.
2. Henry Blid, *Education by the People: Study Circles* (Ludvika, Sweden: Brunnsviksskolorna, 1983), pp. 7-12.
3. Ibid., p. 2.
4. Ibid., pp. 3-4.
5. The Swedish Institute, "Adult Education in Sweden," in *Fact Sheets on Sweden* (Stockholm: The Swedish Institute, December 1982), p. 2.
6. Ibid.

CHAPTER 2

1. Allan Sundqvist, *New Rules for Swedish Study Circles* (Stockholm: National Swedish Federation of Adult Education Associations [SFHL], 1983), p. 7.

2. Often the study organizer's tasks are defined by the collective bargaining agreement, with organizing permitted during work hours. Ulf-Göran Widqvist of Brevskolan said, "The Swedish labor movement depends on the study circle to provide information to union members, to improve educational levels, and to provide the nucleus of campaign workers for political campaigns."

3. The Social Democratic party (SAP) dominated Swedish politics from 1932 until 1976, when a coalition of the Liberal, Center, and Conservative (moderate) parties won and held power until the SAP regained the government in 1982. For a fuller description of Sweden's political movements, see Frances G. Castles, *The Social Democratic Image of Society* (London: Routledge & Kegan Paul, 1978).

CHAPTER 3

1. Norman D. Kurland, "The Scandinavian Study Circle: An Idea for the U.S.," in *Lifelong Learning: The Adult Years* 5, (February 1982): 24.
2. Blid, *Education by the People,* pp. 23-28.
3. National Swedish Board of Education, *Equal Educational Opportunities?* (Stockholm: National Swedish Board of Education, 1983), pp. 10-11.
4. SFHL, *Folkbildningsarbetet,* special issue, *The Study Associations in Sweden* (Stockholm: SFHL, 1976), p. 35.
5. Brevskolan, *The Study Circle,* p. 17.
6. Blid, *Education by the People,* p. 85.
7. SFHL, *Folkbildningsarbetet,* p. 18.
8. Norman Eiger, "The Workplace as Classroom for Democracy: The Swedish Experience," *New York University Education Quarterly* 13, 4 (1982): 16-23.
9. Gosta Vestlund, *Hur Vårder Vi Vår Demokriti?* [How Do We Care for Democracy?] (Stockholm:

National Swedish Board of Education, 1981).
10. SFHL, *Folkbildningsarbetet*, p. 34.

CHAPTER 4
1. SFHL, *Folkbildningsarbetet*, p. 40.
2. A. Dyring and B.E. Vedin, *The Kalla Series: A New Publication Model for Scientific Information* (Stockholm: Swedish Council for Planning and Coordination of Research, 1983).
3. Adult Schools Association (SV), *Introducing SV* (Stockholm: SV, 1977), p. 5.
4. National Educational Association for the YWCA and YMCA (KFUK/M), *This Is the YWCA-YMCA of Sweden* (Stockholm: KFUK/M, 1982), p. 10.
5. Swedish Radio AB, *Swedish Broadcasting Corporation* (Stockholm: Swedish Radio AB, 1979), p. 5.
6. Eiger, "The Workplace as Classroom," p. 20.
7. Ibid., p. 21.
8. Ibid.
9. Budd E. Hall, "Development Campaigns in Rural Tanzania," *Contact*, special series no. 3 (1980).
10. Anders I. Johnsson, Kjell Nyström, and Rolf Sundén, *Adult Education in Tanzania* (Stockholm: Swedish International Development Authority, 1982), p. 5.

CHAPTER 5
1. Jan Byström, *Alla "Studiecirklar" Blir Inte Studiecirklar* [All Study Circles Are Not Study Circles] (Stockholm: University of Stockholm, 1976), see pp. 303-313 for the English summary.
2. Ibid., p. 308.
3. Committee on Methods Testing in Adult Education, *Extended Adult Education: Outreaching Work and Study Circles* (Stockholm: Liber Tryck, 1974).
4. Sundqvist, *New Rules for Swedish Study Circles*, pp. 10-11.

5. Bengt Goranssön, "Some Aspects of Swedish Cultural Policy, from the Standpoint of the Swedish Popular Movements" (Paper presented to the "Scandinavia Today: Cultural Outreach" program, George Meany Center for Labor Studies, Silver Spring, Md., November 1982).
6. T. Stockfeldt and M. Sköld, *Everyday Learning: The Basis of Adult Education* (Stockholm: Brevskolan, 1981), pp. 30-32.
7. Paulo Friere, *Pedagogy of the Oppressed* (London: Herder & Herder, 1970).
8. Paulo Friere, "Education as Cultural Action," in *Conscientization for Liberation,* ed. L. Colonnese (Washington, D.C.: United States Catholic Conference, 1971), pp. 109-122.
9. Kurland, *The Scandinavian Study Circle,* p. 27.
10. Ibid.
11. L.P. Oliver, *The Art of Citizenship: Public Issues Forums* (Dayton, Ohio: Kettering Foundation, 1983), p. 34.

CHAPTER 6

1. Oliver, *The Art of Citizenship,* p. 11. Mr. Studebaker was 100 years old on 10 June 1987 and was the subject of an extensive interview I did in April 1985. See L.P. Oliver, "The American Way Revisited," in *Kettering Review* (Spring 1986): 26-34.
2. Oliver, "Chautauqua and the State Humanities Programs," p. 12.
3. See C.O. Houle, *The Design of Education* (San Francisco: Jossey-Bass, 1976), chap. 2 for an excellent description of the "group dynamics" movement in the United States.
4. Kurland, "The Scandinavian Study Circle."
5. Ibid., p. 27.
6. Ibid., p. 30.

CHAPTER 7

1. David Mathews, "We the People . . . ," *National Forum* 64, 4 (Fall 1984): 46-48, 63-64.
2. Domestic Policy Association (DPA), *The Study Circle in the National Issues Forum* (Dayton, Ohio: DPA, 1985).
3. Daniel Yankelovich, "How the Public Learns the Public's Business," *Kettering Review* (Winter 1985): 8-10.
4. L.P. Oliver, *The National Issues Forums: Reports from the Field* (Dayton, Ohio: Kettering Foundation, 1986).
5. Anita Fonte, *Overview: Tuscon's 1985 NIF* (Unpublished paper, 1986), p. 3.
6. Carl Eschels, *The Dream Becomes a Reality* (Unpublished paper, 1986), pp. 13-14.
7. DPA, "Study Circle Forums in Nebraska," *DPA Newsletter,* February 1986, p. 3.
8. International Union of Bricklayers and Allied Craftsmen (BAC), *Project 2000 Committee Report and Recommendations* (Washington, D.C.: BAC, 1985), p. viii.
9. BAC, *Project 2000,* p. 83.
10. BAC, *Building Union Democracy,* final report of the 1986 BAC Study Circle Program (Washington, D.C.: BAC, 1986), pp. 23-24.
11. Ibid., p. 10.

CHAPTER 8

1. Mathews, "We the People," p. 48.
2. ABF, *Workers' Education in Sweden,* p. 1.

APPENDIX: List of Interviews

Jan Ahltorp, Education Director
Social Democratic party, Stockholm

Lena Årman
Liber Hermods, Malmö

Irina Blid
Brunnsvik College, Ludvika

Rune Blomqvist, President
Foundation for the Promotion
   of Literature, Stockholm

Patrick Breslin
Worker's Educational Association
   (ABF), Stockholm

Agneta Charpentier
Section of Adult Education
Ministry of Education and
   Cultural Affairs, Stockholm

Olle Edelholm, Secretary-General
Nordic Association of Adult
   Education, Lidingö

Peter Engberg,
Associate Secretary-General
National Swedish Federation of
   Adult Education Associations
   (SFHL), Stockholm

Agneta Flinck, Research Assistant
Department of Education
University of Lund, Lund

Rune Flinck, Associate Professor
Department of Education
University of Lund, Lund

Sven-Eric Henricson
Division of Adult Education
National Swedish Board of
   Education, Stockholm

Anders Höglund, Director
Extra-Mural Board of Stockholm
   University, Stockholm

Leif Kindblom, Director
Study Promotion Association (Sfr)
Stockholm

Leif Klint
Study Department
Salaried Employees Educational
   Association (TBV), Stockholm

Eddie Levin
International Relations
Swedish Educational Broadcasting
   Company (UR), Stockholm

Ellen Lind
Adult Schools Association (SV)
Stockholm

Ulrika Malmström, Adviser
Adult Schools Association (SV)
Stockholm

S. A. Mayombwe
Education Administration
Rubondo, Tanzania

Inger Olsson, Information Chief
Skådebanan, Stockholm

Rune Ovik, Managing Director
Foundation for the Promotion
of Literature, Stockholm

Leif Pettersson, Ombudsman
Department of Education
Swedish Confederation of Trade
Unions (LO), Stockholm

Lena Samuelsson
Educational Adviser
National Educational Association
for the YWCA and YMCA
KFUK/M), Stockholm

Gunilla Sterner-Kumm
Swedish Educational Broadcasting
Company (UR), Stockholm

Torbjörn Strandberg, Director
Brunnsvik College, Ludvika

Rolf Theorin, Director Programs
Central Organization of Folk Parks
Stockholm

Lars Ulvenstam
Swedish Broadcasting Corporation
(SR), Stockholm

Gosta Vestlund
Nacka

Ulf-Göran Widqvist, Editor
Brevskolan, Stockholm

SWEDISH INSTITUTE OFFICIALS

Anders Clasen, Director

Ingegerd Grundstedt, Director
Department for Education and Research

Monica Fägerborn
Cecilia Reimers
Program Coordinators

INDEX

A

ABF (Arbetarnas Bildningsförbund), 4, 9; areas of concern, 11,
12, 32, 43; *Fonstret* (The Window),
11; materials, 32, 34-35, 52;
national issue campaigns and, 46,
49, 50; organization, 15; participants, 11-12, 26; SAP and, 4, 11,
26, 50, 51; size, 11, 15; study
circles, 4, 11-12, 15, 17, 33-35, 50,
51, 52, 55, 56, 57, 64; subsidies to,
12, 15. *See also* Brevskolan
Adams, Sam, "Committees of
Correspondence," 90
Addams, Jane, 92
adult education in Sweden, xv, 25-
26, 41, 43, 74, 80-81, 142, 143;
declining civic consciousness and,
71-73, 78; formats, ix, xv-xvi, 74;
historical background, 1-4;
pedagogy (methodology), xvii-
xviii, 21-23, 38; philosophy
(theory), ix, xvi-xvii, 144; popular
movements and, 2-5, 31, 41, 67,
70-71, 102; social purpose, ix,
xvii, xviii, 1, 10, 70-71, 72-73.
See also national educational
associations; study circles in
Sweden
adult education in the United
States, x, 21, 72, 79, 146-147;
BAC Study Circle Program, 120-
140; historical background, 89-
100; media and, 96, 97, 98, 99;
National Issues Forums, 106-120;
small group discussion, 100-104
Adult Schools Association. *See* SV

AFL-CIO, "The Changing Situa-
tion of Workers and Their
Unions," 121
Agricultural Cooperative Exten-
sion programs (U.S.), 74, 91-92,
103
Ahltorp, Jan, 11, 35, 48, 51, 71-72
Allen, Ray, 129, 133
American Association of Com-
munity and Junior Colleges
(AACJC), 98-99
American Foundation for Continu-
ing Education, 95-96
American Issues Forum, 97-98
American Library Association
(ALA), 95, 100; "American
Heritage Project," 95
American Philosophical Society, 90
Anderson, Val, 130
"Annual Educational Leave Act"
(1975), 31
Aquiline, Mike, 128
Armstrong, William, 133, 137

B

BAC Study Circle Program, xi,
120, 121; assessments of (IU),
129; leaders, 120, 122, 125-126,
132-133; make-up of participants,
122, 133; materials, 122, 123, 125,
134-135, 138; nature of, 122, 125;
objectives, xi, 120, 121, 123,
124, 125, 138-139; pedagogy
(methodology), 122, 125-126,

About the Author

Leonard P. Oliver, formerly special assistant to the chairman of the National
Endowment for the Humanities, is now
director of the five-year-old public policy
consulting firm of Oliver Associates in
Washington, D.C. His long-standing interests in adult education as an instrument
for social change sparked his visit to Sweden
in 1984 on a Swedish Government Bicentennial Fellowship to analyze Swedish adult
education, and he chaired the Work Group
on Adult Civic Education at the 1985 World
Assembly on Adult Education in Buenos
Aires. In addition, he is currently engaged
with the Kettering Foundation in research-
ing and developing the Domestic Policy Association and the National Issues Forum,
and he also directs the Study Circle Program of the International Union of Bricklayers and Allied Craftsmen. Dr. Oliver,
who holds a Ph.D. in adult education from
the University of Chicago, is a former Olym-
pic soccer player who remains active as both
a clinician and a coach.